W9-DJC-051

Writing

ISBN-13: 978-1-4190-3415-2
ISBN-10: 1-4190-3415-4

The paper used in this book comes from sustainable resources.

Steck
Vaughn™
A Harcourt Achieve Imprint

Printed in the United States of America.
2 3 4 5 6 7 8 862 13 12 11 10 09

www.HarcourtSchoolSupply.com
1-800-531-5015

Core Skills Writing
Grade 5

Contents 2
Introduction. 4
Features. 5
Skills Correlation 7
Writing Rubric. 8

Unit 1: Laying the Foundation

Why Write? 9
What to Write 10
Keeping a Journal 12
Primary Parts of Speech 13
Modifiers 15
Connectives 16
The Writing Process 17
The Seven Traits of Good Writing 19
Basic Rules of Writing 22

Unit 2: Building Sentences

What Is a Sentence? 24
The Main Idea of a Sentence 25
Subject-Verb Agreement 26
Direct Objects 27
Helping Verbs 28
Linking Verbs 29
Review: The Main Idea of a Sentence . . . 30
Adding Details to Sentences 31
Expanding Sentences with Adjectives . . . 32
Appealing to the Reader's Senses 33
Expanding Sentences with Adverbs 34
Negatives 35
Review: Modifiers 36
Clauses and Phrases 37
Expanding Sentences with
    Prepositional Phrases 39
Expanding Sentences with
    Coordinate Conjunctions 41
Compound Subjects 42
Compound Predicates 43
Agreement of Verbs and
    Compound Subjects 44
Subordinate Conjunctions 45
Review: Connectives 46
Kinds of Sentences 47
End Punctuation 49
Simple, Compound, and
    Complex Sentences 50
Using Commas 51
Combining Sentences 52
Combining Sentences with the Same
    Subject or Predicate 53
Review: Working with Sentences 54
Active and Passive Verbs 55
Verb Tense 56
Writing Descriptive Sentences 57
Using Figurative Language 60
Sentence Beginnings 62
Sentence Lengths 63
Sentence Errors: Fragments 64
Sentence Errors: Run-on Sentences 65
Seeing Your Writing 67
Self-Evaluation: What's Going On? 68

Unit 3: Building Paragraphs

What Is a Paragraph? 69
What Is in a Paragraph? 70
Writing a Topic Sentence 71
Writing Detail Sentences 72
Writing a Concluding Sentence 73
Using Time Order in Paragraphs 74
Prewriting a Paragraph 75
Voice 76
Writing Pattern: Main Idea
  and Details 77
Writing Pattern: Summary 78
Writing Pattern: Sequence
  of Events 79
Writing Pattern: Compare
  and Contrast 80
Writing Pattern: Cause and Effect 81
Writing Pattern: Problem
  and Solution 82
Keeping to the Topic 83
Revising 84
Proofreading a Paragraph 85
Publishing 86
Self-Evaluation: What's Going On? 87

Unit 4: Writing Forms

Writing a Descriptive Paragraph:
  Person 88
Writing a Descriptive Paragraph:
  Place 89
Writing a Descriptive Paragraph:
  Thing 90
Writing a Narrative Paragraph 91
Personal Narrative 92
Dialogue 93
Writing a Comparison and
  Contrast Paragraph 94
Planning the Comparison and
  Contrast Paragraph 95
Writing a Persuasive Paragraph 96
Writing a How-to Paragraph 99
Writing an Information Paragraph 101
Writing a Book Report 104
Writing an Informative Report 106

Taking Notes 107
Direct Quotes 108
A Writing Plan: Outlining 109
Beginning and Ending a Report 111
Writing Your Report 112

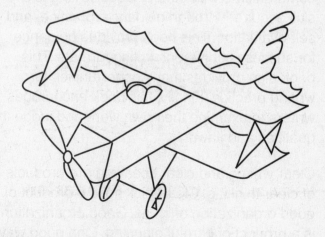

Blackline Masters

Prewriting Survey 113
Writing Traits Checklist 115
Proofreading Checklist 117
Proofreading Marks 118
Self-Evaluation Checklist 119
Sentence Graphic Organizers 120
Main Idea and Details Web 121
Summary Chart 122
Problem and Solution Chart 123
Cause and Effect Chart 123
Paragraph Structure Chart 124

Glossary 125
Answer Key 127

Introduction

Writing is one of the core skills necessary for success in school and in life. The better writer a person is, the better that person can communicate with others. Good writing is a skill acquired through guidance, practice, and self-evaluation. This book provides guidance for success in different writing formats. This book also provides many opportunities for writing practice. Finally, this book encourages writers to examine their own work and judge its qualities and flaws.

Clear writing and clear speaking are products of clear thinking. Clear thinking is a product of good organization of ideas. Good organization is a product of careful planning. One good way to plan is through graphic organizers.

- In this book, different kinds of graphic organizers are provided for students to plan their writing.
- One kind of graphic organizer, emphasized in Unit 2, allows writers to "see" their writing clearly.
- By "seeing" their writing, students can more easily determine how the different parts of a sentence work together to produce a clear expression of their main idea.
- This kind of graphic organizer allows students a more visual and tactile appreciation of their writing. It also appeals to multiple intelligences.

Language Arts Standards

The National Council of Teachers of English (NCTE) believes that "all students must have the opportunities and resources to develop the language skills they need to pursue life's goals and to participate fully as informed, productive members of society." The NCTE also feels that students must "apply a wide range of strategies as they write and use different writing process elements appropriately to communicate with different audiences for a variety of purposes." The Skills Correlation Chart on page 7 allows easy location of these skills and strategies in the book.

Organization

This book is divided into four units. Each unit builds upon earlier units. Using this scaffolded approach, writing becomes like construction. This book can help to build better writers.

- **Unit 1: Laying the Foundation** addresses basic concepts of writing, such as good writing traits and the process of writing.
- **Unit 2: Building Sentences** emphasizes the act of writing. Writers first deal with the main idea of a sentence, and then expand sentences by adding other parts of speech. By using graphic organizers, writers can visualize their sentences clearly.
- **Unit 3: Building Paragraphs** focuses on the structure and content of a well-written paragraph. Writers also learn about revising, proofreading, and self-evaluation in this unit.
- **Unit 4: Writing Forms** provides guidance and opportunities to practice writing in different formats such as narration, description, persuasion, and informative reports.

Write Away

For too many students, writing is a struggle or a pain. They may not realize the benefits of being a good writer, or they may not care. This book tries to reach out to all writers with a light tone and an approach that allows students to "see" their writing in a new light. Writing does not have to be a chore. It can be fun. Students just have to be reminded that good writing can be their golden ticket to success in school and life.

Features

The title clearly identifies the skill.

Bullets highlight important points of the skill.

Examples model the skill.

Students creatively apply the skill in **Write Away.**

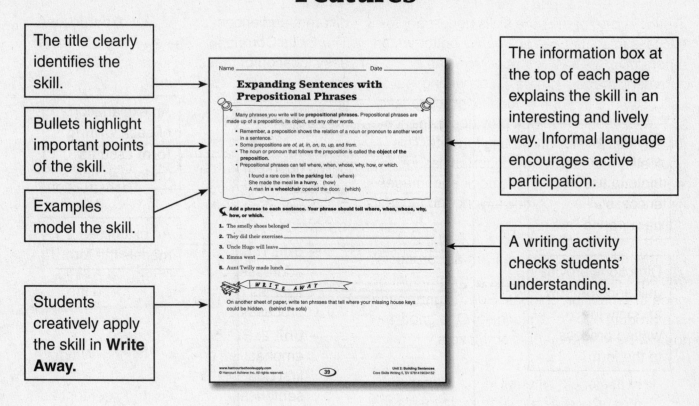

Expanding Sentences with Prepositional Phrases

Many phrases you write will be **prepositional phrases**. Prepositional phrases are made up of a preposition, its object, and any other words.

- Remember, a preposition shows the relation of a noun or pronoun to another word in a sentence.
- Some prepositions are *of*, *at*, *in*, *on*, *to*, *up*, and *from*.
- The noun or pronoun that follows the preposition is called the **object of the preposition.**
- Prepositional phrases can tell where, when, whose, why, how, or which.

I found a rare coin **in the parking lot.**   (where)
She made the meal **in a hurry.**   (how)
A man **in a wheelchair** opened the door.   (which)

Add a phrase to each sentence. Your phrase should tell where, when, whose, why, how, or which.

1. The smelly shoes belonged _____
2. They did their exercises _____
3. Uncle Hugo will leave _____
4. Emma went _____
5. Aunt Twilly made lunch _____

WRITE AWAY

On another sheet of paper, write ten phrases that tell where your missing house keys could be hidden.   (behind the sofa)

www.harcourtschoolsupply.com
© Harcourt Achieve Inc. All rights reserved.
39
Unit 2: Building Sentences
Core Skills Writing 5, SV 9781419034152

The information box at the top of each page explains the skill in an interesting and lively way. Informal language encourages active participation.

A writing activity checks students' understanding.

Checklists guide students through the writing process.

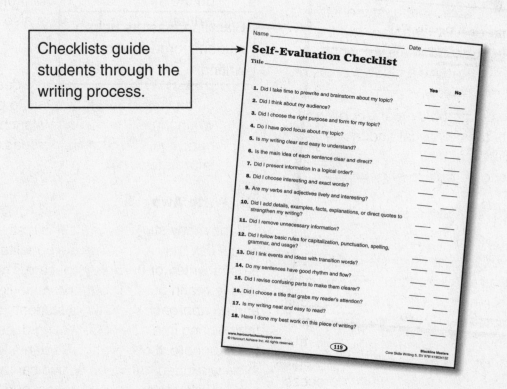

Self-Evaluation Checklist

Title _____

	Yes	No
1. Did I take time to prewrite and brainstorm about my topic?		
2. Did I think about my audience?		
3. Did I choose the right purpose and form for my topic?		
4. Do I have good focus about my topic?		
5. Is my writing clear and easy to understand?		
6. Is the main idea of each sentence clear and direct?		
7. Did I present information in a logical order?		
8. Did I choose interesting and exact words?		
9. Are my verbs and adjectives lively and interesting?		
10. Did I add details, examples, facts, explanations, or direct quotes to strengthen my writing?		
11. Did I remove unnecessary information?		
12. Did I follow basic rules for capitalization, punctuation, spelling, grammar, and usage?		
13. Did I link events and ideas with transition words?		
14. Do my sentences have good rhythm and flow?		
15. Did I revise confusing parts to make them clearer?		
16. Did I choose a title that grabs my reader's attention?		
17. Is my writing neat and easy to read?		
18. Have I done my best work on this piece of writing?		

www.harcourtschoolsupply.com
© Harcourt Achieve Inc. All rights reserved.
119
Blackline Masters
Core Skills Writing 5, SV 9781419034152

Features

Bullets identify specific writing hints to assure successful paragraphs.

Directions provide guidance on how to apply the writing process to the form.

An explanation of each **writing form** assures understanding.

An example models the form.

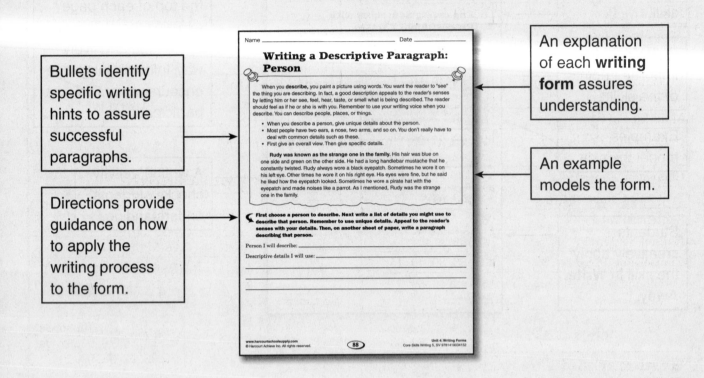

Name _____ Date _____

Writing a Descriptive Paragraph: Person

When you **describe**, you paint a picture using words. You want the reader to "see" the thing you are describing. In fact, a good description appeals to the reader's senses by letting him or her see, feel, hear, taste, or smell what is being described. The reader should feel as if he or she is with you. Remember to use your writing voice when you describe. You can describe people, places, or things.

• When you describe a person, give unique details about the person.
• Most people have two ears, a nose, two arms, and so on. You don't really have to deal with common details such as these.
• First give an overall view. Then give specific details.

   Rudy was known as the strange one in the family. His hair was blue on one side and green on the other side. He had a long handlebar mustache that he constantly twisted. Rudy always wore a black eyepatch. Sometimes he wore it on his left eye. Other times he wore it on his right eye. His eyes were fine, but he said he liked how the eyepatch looked. Sometimes he wore a pirate hat with the eyepatch and made noises like a parrot. As I mentioned, Rudy was the strange one in the family.

   First choose a person to describe. Next write a list of details you might use to describe that person. Remember to use unique details. Appeal to the reader's senses with your details. Then, on another sheet of paper, write a paragraph describing that person.

Person I will describe: _____

Descriptive details I will use: _____

_____

_____

_____

88

Unit 4: Writing Forms
Core Skills Writing 5, SV 9781419034152

Blackline masters help students organize their writing.

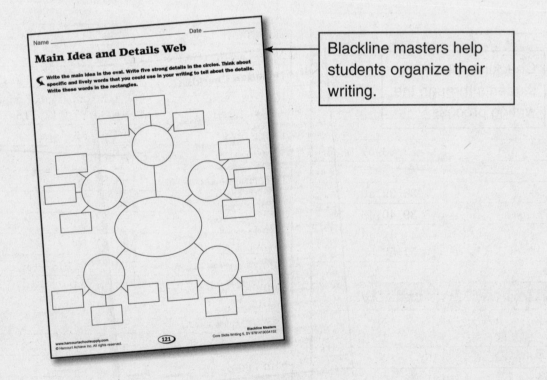

Name _____ Date _____

Main Idea and Details Web

Write the main idea in the oval. Write five strong details in the circles. Think about specific and lively words that you could use in your writing to tell about the details. Write these words in the rectangles.

121

Blackline Masters
Core Skills Writing 5, SV 9781419034152

Skills Correlation

Skill	Page
Vocabulary	
Word Choice	20, 32, 33, 57, 58
Figurative Language	60, 61
Sentences	
Word Order in Sentences	62
Recognizing Sentences and Sentence Types	47, 48, 49, 50
Main Idea of Sentence	25, 30
Subjects and Predicates	25, 26, 27, 28, 29, 30, 42, 43, 44, 46, 53
Compound Sentences	50
Sentence Combining	52, 53, 54
Sentence Fragments	64
Run-on Sentences	65, 66
Clauses and Phrases	37, 38, 39, 40, 45
Compound Subjects and Predicates	42, 43, 44, 53
Objects	27, 30
Sentence Variety	57, 58, 59, 62, 63
Grammar and Usage	
Common and Proper Nouns	13
Singular and Plural Nouns	13
Possessive Nouns	13
Verbs and Verb Tense	14, 56
Subject-Verb Agreement	26, 44
Verb Phrases	28
Active and Passive Voice Verbs	14, 55
Pronouns	13
Adjectives	15, 32, 33, 57, 58, 59
Adverbs	15, 34
Prepositions	16, 38, 39, 40
Prepositional Phrases	38, 39, 40, 46
Conjunctions	16, 41, 42, 43, 45, 46, 51, 52, 53
Double Negatives	35
Capitalization and Punctuation	
Capitalization: First Word in Sentence	24
Capitalization: Proper Nouns	13
End Punctuation	47, 48, 49
Commas	51, 52, 54
Quotation Marks	93, 108

Skill	Page
Composition	
Expanding Sentences	31, 32, 33, 34, 36, 39, 40, 41, 52, 54
Paragraphs: Topic Sentence (main idea)	69, 70, 71, 75, 77, 121
Paragraphs: Supporting Details	69, 70, 72, 77, 124
Paragraphs: Concluding Sentence	69, 70, 73, 124
Time Order in Paragraphs	74
Writing Process	
Audience	10, 18, 20, 21, 113, 114
Purpose	11, 113, 114
Voice	20, 76
Prewriting and Brainstorming	17, 75, 113, 114
Topic	17, 19, 22, 83
Organization and Form	11, 19, 77, 78, 79, 80, 81, 82, 88, 89, 90, 91, 92, 94, 95, 96, 97, 98, 99, 100, 101, 102, 103, 104, 105, 106, 109, 110, 111, 112, 113, 114, 121, 122, 123, 124
Outlining	109, 110
Note Taking	107, 108
Drafting	17, 23
Revising and Proofreading	18, 21, 23, 64, 65, 66, 68, 84, 85, 87, 117, 118, 119
Publishing	18, 21, 86
Types of Writing	
Descriptive Paragraph	88, 89, 90
How-to Paragraph	99, 100
Narrative Paragraph	91, 92, 93
Persuasive Paragraph	96, 97, 98
Information Paragraph	101, 102, 103
Comparing and Contrasting	80, 94, 95
Cause and Effect	81, 123
Problem and Solution	82, 123
Summary	78, 104, 122
Book Report	104, 105
Informative Report	106, 107, 108, 109, 111, 112

Writing Rubric

Score of 4

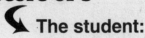 **The student:**

- <u>clearly and completely</u> addresses the writing task,
- demonstrates an understanding of the purpose for writing,
- maintains a single focus,
- presents a main idea supported by relevant details,
- uses paragraphs to organize main ideas and supporting ideas under the umbrella of a thesis statement,
- presents content in a logical order and sequence,
- uses variety in sentence beginnings and length,
- chooses the correct writing pattern and form to communicate ideas clearly,
- clearly portrays feelings through voice and word choice,
- uses language appropriate to the writing task, such as language rich in sensory details in a descriptive passage,
- uses vocabulary to suit purpose and audience,
- summarizes main ideas in a concluding paragraph when appropriate, such as in an informative report,
- establishes and defends a position in a persuasive paragraph, and
- has few or no errors in the standard rules of English grammar, punctuation, capitalization, and spelling.

Score of 3

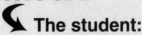 **The student:**

- <u>generally</u> follows the criteria described above, and
- has some errors in the standard rules of English grammar, punctuation, capitalization, and spelling, but not enough to impair the reader's comprehension.

Score of 2

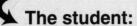 **The student:**

- <u>marginally</u> follows the criteria described above, and
- has several errors in the standard rules of English grammar, punctuation, capitalization, and spelling that may impair a reader's comprehension.

Score of 1

The student:

- <u>fails</u> to follow the criteria described above, and
- has many errors in the standard rules of English grammar, punctuation, capitalization, and spelling that impair a reader's comprehension.

www.harcourtschoolsupply.com
© Harcourt Achieve Inc. All rights reserved.

Writing Rubric
Core Skills Writing 5, SV 9781419034152

Why Write?

Do you like to write? Many people don't. They think they can speak everything they need to communicate. Can they? Maybe, but sometimes writing is better than talking.

- When you write, you have more time to think.
- You can organize your ideas better.
- You can make your ideas more permanent by writing them on paper.
- Writing takes your place when you are not there to talk.

Writing is really much like talking. When you write or talk, you use ideas. You use the different parts of speech. You often use complete sentences. And your goal is the same for both methods—to communicate with others. Writing can be fun, too. Just think, in twenty or thirty years you can read something you wrote in the fifth grade. Won't that be funny?

Darken the circle by the answer that best completes each sentence.

1. When you write, you have time to _____ your ideas better.

   (A) organize   (B) erase

   (C) forget   (D) mix up

2. You have time to _____ before you write your ideas on paper.

   (A) buy bananas   (B) find your pen

   (C) think   (D) nap

3. You can make your ideas _____ by writing them on paper.

   (A) invisible   (B) goofier

   (C) more permanent (D) wrong

4. Writing can take your _____ when you aren't available to talk.

   (A) sandwich   (B) place

   (C) bicycle   (D) money

Do you like writing or talking better? Discuss your ideas with a friend or family member. Then, in your best writing, tell which you like and why. Use another sheet of paper.

What to Write

To be a good writer, you have to think about what you write. Sometimes you have an assignment to write. Sometimes you must give someone directions. Sometimes you want to write a list or a poem. There are many things you can write. Before you do, though, you must make three decisions.

1. **Who is your audience?** Your audience is your reader. Are you writing for yourself? Your friends or family? A newspaper? Your community? Before you write, ask yourself questions to target your audience.

   - Who will read what I write?
   - What do I know about these people?
   - What do I have to say to the readers?
   - Why do I want the readers to care about my writing?
   - Am I writing about my feelings or about facts?
   - Will my writing be funny or serious?

Name a possible audience for each piece of writing.

1. a happy poem about your dreams

   _____

2. a report about litter problems

   _____

3. an invitation to a dance

   _____

4. a movie review

   _____

 W R I T E   A W A Y

Would a letter you write to the governor of your state be different from a letter you write to a friend? Why or why not? How would the letters be different? Discuss your ideas with a friend or family member. Write a few sentences about your ideas.

_____

_____

_____

_____

_____

What to Write, page 2

2. **Why are you writing?** You must choose a purpose, or goal, for your writing. Writers have four main purposes:

   - to **express** personal feelings or ideas (diary, journal)
   - to **inform** (list, report, research paper)
   - to **entertain** others (story, poem, joke)
   - to **persuade** others (speech, book review)

3. **How will you organize your writing?** Your audience and your purpose determine your form. To be an effective writer, you must choose the correct form to achieve your purpose. This book presents many forms you can use to write.

What purpose would you use to write each of the following? Darken the circle by your choice.

1. your feelings about a favorite relative

   (A) express   (B) entertain

   (C) persuade   (D) inform

2. a funny story about whales

   (A) express   (B) entertain

   (C) persuade   (D) inform

3. a report about Benjamin Franklin

   (A) express   (B) entertain

   (C) persuade   (D) inform

4. a speech for a city election

   (A) express   (B) entertain

   (C) persuade   (D) inform

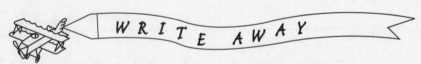

WRITE AWAY

You want to stay up later on Saturday night. How can you make this happen?

What purpose would you use? _____

Who would your audience be? _____

Name _____ Date _____

Keeping a Journal

Jour is a French word that means "day." A **journal** is a record of daily events. In a journal, you can write about your ideas and thoughts. You can write about your feelings and hopes. You can write stories or poems in your journal. And journals can be fun to read when you get older. You can make your journal better by doing these things.

- Write the date.
- Write about important events that happened today.
- Tell why the events are important to you.
- Write poems or stories about the events. Draw pictures.

Here's a sample:

October 14, 2007   My dad and I went fishing this morning. The weather was really cold, and the fish weren't biting. When we were about to give up, I felt a tug on my line. I hooked the biggest fish I had ever seen. The fish didn't want to be caught, either. Finally, after about twenty minutes, I pulled in the fish. Dad said it would make a good supper. It was a neat day.

> **Write a short journal entry about something important that happened to you today. Use another sheet of paper if necessary.**

TODAY IS

_____

_____

_____

_____

_____

_____

W R I T E   A W A Y

Start your own journal. Use notebook paper. Write the date. Write your feelings and ideas. Write poems and stories about your daily life. The entries can be words that only you know about. Writing your personal feelings can help you understand them better.

Unit 1: Laying the Foundation
Core Skills Writing 5, SV 9781419034152

Primary Parts of Speech

Two of the most important parts of speech are **nouns** and **pronouns.** Nouns and pronouns name things. A noun is a word that names a person, place, or thing.

- A **common noun** names any person, place, or thing (boy, library, book). It begins with a small letter.
- A **proper noun** names a specific person, place, or thing (Emily, New York, Statue of Liberty). It begins with a capital letter.
- Nouns can be singular, plural, or possessive.

Pronouns take the place of nouns. Use pronouns to avoid repeating words.

- A **subject pronoun** is used as the subject of a sentence (I, we, he, she).
- An **object pronoun** is used as the object of a sentence (me, them, him, her).
- Pronouns can be singular, plural, or possessive (it, they, my).

 Write nouns or pronouns to fit each writing need.

1. What nouns could you use to write about the library?

_____

2. What nouns could you use to write about the mall?

_____

3. What pronouns could you use to write about yourself?

_____

4. What pronouns could you use to write about your friends?

_____

On another sheet of paper, write a list of twenty common nouns. Beside each noun, write a pronoun that might take its place.

Primary Parts of Speech, page 2

A **verb** is another important part of speech. A verb shows action or connects the subject to another word in a sentence. Verbs can be **action verbs, linking verbs,** or **helping verbs.** Verbs can be singular or plural. They can be active or passive.

Verbs are also used to tell the time something is happening. The time a verb shows is called **tense.**

- A **present tense verb** tells what is happening now.
- A **past tense verb** tells what happened in the past.
- A **future tense verb** tells what will happen in the future.

present	past	future
smell	smelled	will smell

 Write verbs to fit each writing need.

1. What verbs could you use to write about playing a ballgame?

_____

2. What verbs could you use to write about what you do during the night?

_____

3. What verbs could you use to write about schoolwork you must do?

_____

4. What verbs could you use to write about a vacation last year?

_____

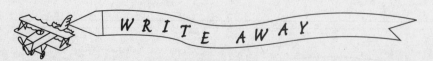

WRITE AWAY

What are some verbs that tell how you can use your mouth? (chew, speak) On another sheet of paper, write a list of all the verbs you can think of.

Unit 1: Laying the Foundation
Core Skills Writing 5, SV 9781419034152

Name _____ Date _____

Modifiers

Adjectives and **adverbs** are two more parts of speech. Adjectives and adverbs are **modifiers.** A modifier is a word or group of words that changes the meaning of another word.

cow ⟶ **blue** cow

- An adjective modifies a noun or pronoun.

    cloudy sky   **scary** story   **lucky** him

- An adverb modifies a verb, an adjective, or another adverb.

    chewed **slowly**   **very** tired   **quite** smoothly

Write adjectives or adverbs to fit each writing need.

1. What adjectives could you use to write about winter?

_____

2. What adjectives could you use to write about thunder?

_____

3. What adjectives could you use to write about your neighborhood?

_____

4. What adverbs could you use to write about the way you sing?

_____

5. What adverbs could you use to write about the way people dance?

_____

On another sheet of paper, draw a picture. You can use a pencil, a pen, or crayons. Then write at least ten adjectives to describe your picture.

Unit 1: Laying the Foundation
Core Skills Writing 5, SV 9781419034152

Name _____ Date _____

Connectives

Conjunctions and prepositions are two more parts of speech. Conjunctions and prepositions are **connectives.** Connectives join parts of a sentence.

- A conjunction connects words or groups of words. Some common conjunctions are *and, or, but,* and *yet.*

    day **and** night   right **or** wrong

- A preposition shows the relation of a noun or pronoun to another word in a sentence. Some common prepositions are *of, at, in, on, to, up, near, from, by,* and *into.*

    The bird is **in** the tree.

Draw a line between each conjunction and its meaning.

1. but   a choice between two things

2. and   a difference between two things

3. or   addition of two things

4. yet   same as *but*

Write two prepositions that have a meaning similar to the given word.

5. near _____

6. under _____

Think of prepositions that tell a location, such as *above.* Write as many as you can.

_____

_____

_____

_____

Core Skills Writing 5, SV 9781419034152

Name _____   Date _____

The Writing Process

Have you ever sat and stared at a blank sheet of paper? Let's face it—sometimes you just can't think of anything to write. But this is not unusual. Many people have the same problem. Luckily, these steps can help you fill that blank paper with wonderful words.

1. Prewriting

Prewriting is sometimes called **brainstorming.** It is the step in which you think about what and why you are writing. You choose a purpose and an audience. You choose a topic and make a list of your ideas. Then you organize your ideas so they make sense. Many writers use outlines or graphic organizers. The Prewriting Survey on pages 113 and 114 can help you plan your writing.

2. Drafting

In the drafting step, writers put their ideas on paper. They write words, ideas, and sentences. Some parts of the draft may have too much information. Other parts may not have enough information. There are often many mistakes in this step of the writing process. But that's OK! A draft is not supposed to be perfect. You just want to get all of your ideas on paper. You concentrate on what you want to say. You can fix your mistakes later.

↰ **Suppose you must eat a bug sandwich for lunch. You decide to write about it in your journal. Use the organizer to help you prewrite.**

Nouns I might use: _____

Verbs I might use: _____

Adjectives I might use: _____

Adverbs I might use: _____

W R I T E   A W A Y

Use the words above to write a few sentences about eating the bug sandwich.

_____

_____

_____

_____

The Writing Process, page 2

3. Revising

Revising means "seeing again." In the revising step, you "see" your draft again. Read your work to be sure it makes sense. You may find new ways to arrange your ideas. You may uncover new ways to express yourself. You can move ideas around. You can remove or add details to make the writing clearer. You can often hear problems when you read your writing aloud. Ask someone else to read your work and give you suggestions for improvement.

4. Proofreading

It is important to proofread your work before you publish it. When you proofread, you look at your writing carefully for mistakes. You should read your work once for capital letters and punctuation. You should read it a second time for spelling. You should read it a third time for verb tense and subject-verb agreement. You should read it a fourth time for sentence structure. You can use the Proofreading Checklist on page 117 as a guide. A list of Proofreading Marks can be found on page 118.

5. Publishing

Publishing is fun. Publishing means "to make public." You can present your writing to your teacher, to your friends, to your family, or to the community. You can read it orally, post it on a Web site, print it in a newspaper, or make it into a book. First, make a clean copy of your writing. You can hand write it or type it on the computer. Then, add pictures, a cover, and a title page if you like. Now the writing is ready to share! What will your audience think?

Read the steps in the writing process. Write numbers 1 through 5 to show the correct order.

_____ Write your first draft. Get your ideas on paper.

_____ Read your writing carefully to be sure it makes sense.

_____ Choose a topic to write about and make notes.

_____ Make a clean copy of your writing to share with others.

_____ Proofread your writing to check for spelling and grammar errors.

Think of different ways you can share your writing with others. Write a list of your ideas.

Name _____ Date _____

The Seven Traits of Good Writing

When you write, you have a **purpose,** or reason, for writing. You might want to inform or entertain your reader. You might try to convince your reader. There are seven **writing traits,** or skills, that will help you achieve your purpose. These writing traits can help you become a better writer.

1. Ideas

You write about your **ideas,** or thoughts on a topic. What you have to say is important. Your ideas are just as good as anyone else's. When you write, you share your ideas. So, you must be sure your ideas make sense. Include enough details to make your ideas clear to the reader. Good ideas show good thinking.

2. Organization

The **organization** of your writing is the way you group your ideas. First, you must choose the correct form of writing for your purpose. E-mail messages, stories, reports, and journals are some writing forms. Next, your writing should have good structure. Are your ideas written in a logical order? Do you have a beginning, a middle, and an end? Do your paragraphs have strong topic sentences? Finally, check your very first sentence. Does it grab the reader's attention? If so, the reader will keep reading. That's important! Where would a writer be without a reader?

➤ **Write a word to complete each sentence.**

1. When you write about your _____, you tell your thoughts on a topic.

2. Seven writing _____ can help you to write better.

3. The way you group ideas in your writing is your _____.

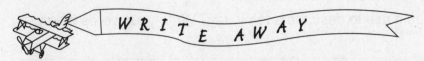
WRITE AWAY

How is a newspaper report like a television news report? How are they different? Brainstorm your ideas with a friend or family member. Then write two or three sentences about your ideas on another sheet of paper.

Unit 1: Laying the Foundation
Core Skills Writing 5, SV 9781419034152

The Seven Traits of Good Writing, page 2

3. Voice

When you talk, people can tell by your voice how you feel. They know if you are happy, sad, or angry. As a writer, you want to let the reader know what you are feeling, too. You use a writing **voice.** To share a happy feeling, you will write about ideas that are happy. You choose words that are happy. When you use the writing trait of voice, you make the reader feel the way you do. Your writing voice replaces your speaking voice.

What voice would you use if someone returned your lost pet? _____

4. Word Choice

You know that you can choose words to make your reader feel a certain way. **Word choice** is important in other ways, too. You must be sure the reader clearly understands what you are writing about. You should choose exact words to explain an idea. Words that appeal to the senses help readers draw a mental picture of your writing.

Write a word to complete each sentence.

4. Use the trait of _____ to make the reader feel the way you do.

5. Exact _____ can help you to explain an idea.

WRITE AWAY

What are some words that you could use to describe a rainy day? Write your words below.

_____

_____

_____

_____

_____

_____

The Seven Traits of Good Writing, page 3

5. Sentence Fluency

Sentence fluency is when the sentences in your text flow smoothly. Your writing has a rhythm. You can achieve this by changing the length of your sentences. You can also write sentences that have different patterns. Read your sentences aloud. Do they flow or stumble?

6. Conventions

The **conventions** are all the rules of grammar and writing. Does each sentence have the correct end punctuation? Is each sentence complete? Are the words spelled correctly? Follow the rules to correct the mistakes in your writing.

7. Presentation

Presentation is the way your words and pictures look on the page. Your work should look neat and clean. It should be easy to read. The pictures should show the most important ideas. And don't forget a good title! A good title makes readers want to read your writing.

Would you want to read a book named Stuff You Shouldn't Know About? Why or why not?

_____

You will use these writing traits all through the writing process. You can use the Writing Traits Checklist on pages 115 and 116 to help you become a better writer.

Write a word to complete each sentence.

6. _____ is the way the words and pictures look on the page.

7. Sentence _____ is when the words in your sentences flow.

8. The _____ are the rules of writing and grammar.

WRITE AWAY

How can a title make a reader want to read a book or watch a movie? What is your favorite title ever? Why did that title make you want to read or watch? Brainstorm your ideas with a friend or family member. Write your ideas on another sheet of paper.

Basic Rules of Writing

When you write, you can let your imagination go crazy. You can think deeply about different topics. You can write about your most personal feelings or create fantasy lands. As a writer, you can change the way you express yourself. You can use different words and experiment with new topics. You never stop learning how to write. It is a fun and rewarding process. Here are a few basic rules to make you a better writer.

Write What You Know

Write about things that interest you, if possible. What kinds of things do you know a lot about? Try writing about one of these topics. You will write better if you understand and feel strongly about your topic. Your reader will know that what you've written is important to you.

Stick to the Topic

Once you choose a topic, you must keep your writing focused on that topic. Decide what your readers need to know about your topic. If you're writing about an animal, focus on what it looks like. Give details about how it acts and what it eats. Don't let your writing wander off to some other topic. One way to stick to the topic is to organize. Make an outline of what you want to write. You can write an outline on paper or create one in your mind.

 **Write a word to complete each sentence.**

1. When you write, your _____ can go crazy.

2. Try to write about topics that _____ you.

3. Keep your writing focused on your _____.

4. One way to stick to the topic is to _____.

5. A good way to organize is to write an _____.

W R I T E   A W A Y

What do you know a lot about? Write a list of topics you know about on another sheet of paper.

Basic Rules of Writing, page 2

Drafts

After you organize, you are ready to write the first draft. You should plan to write two or three drafts. When you write your first draft, you should write as though you are telling a story to your friends. Give all the details, but don't worry about how you sound. Don't worry about mistakes or neatness. The important thing is to put your ideas on paper. You can organize them better in later drafts. You can add or remove details later, too.

Reread and Edit

You don't have to be a perfect speller to be a good writer. You don't need to know all the rules of grammar, either. But you should correct as many errors as you can. Read your work over and over until you have fixed your mistakes. Try reading your work aloud. That way, both your eyes and your ears can help you catch problems. Use the Proofreading Checklist on page 117 to help you find errors. When you have corrected as many problems as you can, you are ready to write your final draft.

 **Write a word to complete each sentence.**

6. After you organize your ideas, you should write your first _____.

7. In your first draft, you shouldn't worry about making _____.

8. Read your work _____ so that your ears can help you catch writing errors.

W R I T E   A W A Y

What are your writing strengths and weaknesses? What are some other ways you can improve your writing? Write your ideas below.

_____

_____

_____

_____

_____

Name _____ Date _____

What Is a Sentence?

A **sentence** is a group of words that tells a complete thought. It begins with a capital letter. A sentence has two main parts, a **subject** and a **predicate**.

- The subject tells who or what the sentence is about.
- The **complete subject** is all the words in the subject.

 Big fish swim in the ocean.

- The predicate tells what the subject is or does.
- The **complete predicate** is all the words in the predicate.

 Big fish **swim in the ocean.**

Are the words below sentences? Write yes or *no*.

_____ **1.** Riley reads reports.

_____ **2.** Jenna juggles.

_____ **3.** Howling hounds here.

_____ **4.** Tito tosses tacos.

Write a word or words on the line to make each sentence complete.

5. _____ buys bananas.

6. _____ writes words.

7. Antonia _____.

8. Eric _____.

W R I T E   A W A Y

On another sheet of paper, write five short sentences like those above. Include a subject or a predicate and a line for the other part. Trade with a friend or family member. Complete each other's sentences.

Unit 2: Building Sentences
Core Skills Writing 5, SV 9781419034152

Name _____   Date _____

The Main Idea of a Sentence

The simple subject and simple predicate form the **main idea** of the sentence.

- The **simple subject** is the main noun or pronoun in the complete subject.
- The **simple predicate** is the main verb in the complete predicate.

Ducks quack.

Ducks	**quack**
subject	predicate

⟵ main idea line

You can use a graphic organizer to make a diagram of the sentence. Separate the subject from the predicate with a bar. Capitalize the first word of the sentence.

Read the poem below. Complete the last two lines of the poem by writing a subject or predicate on the line. Try to make rhymes. Then write two of the sentences in the graphic organizers.

Birds sing.

Tigers pounce.

_____ ring.

Balls _____.

W R I T E   A W A Y

On another sheet of paper, write a poem like the one above. Write your poem about the way animals move (*Frogs hop.*). Then write each sentence in a graphic organizer that you draw.

Name _____ Date _____

Subject-Verb Agreement

The verb you use as a predicate in a sentence must agree in number with the subject.

- Use a **singular verb** when the subject is singular.

   A shark swims. ⬅——— a singular verb for a singular subject

- Use a **plural verb** when the subject is plural.

   Sharks swim. ⬅——— a plural verb for a plural subject

Write a subject or verb as needed to complete each sentence. Be sure that the subject and verb agree in number.

1. Whales _____.

2. Snow _____.

3. Cats _____.

4. A puppy _____.

5. A _____ stinks.

6. _____ sting.

7. _____ flash.

8. The _____ blows.

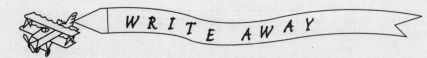
W R I T E   A W A Y

Put your thinking cap on. Some nouns can be singular or plural. One example is *sheep.* How many others can you think of? Write a list below.

_____

_____

_____

_____

_____

_____

Direct Objects

The main idea of your sentence may include a **direct object.** A direct object follows an action verb. It receives the action of the verb. It is part of the complete predicate. The direct object will be a noun or a pronoun.

Kids fly kites.

Kids	fly	kites

With a graphic organizer, you can easily see the main idea of the sentence. A long bar separates the subject from the predicate. A shorter bar separates the predicate from the direct object.

Circle the direct object in each sentence. Then write two of the sentences in the graphic organizers below. Be sure to write the subject, predicate, and object in the correct place.

1. Flora grows flowers.

2. Horses eat hay.

3. Boys catch fish.

4. Emma edited her report.

5. Aron called me today.

6. I wrote a book.

Add an object to complete each sentence.

I want _____.

Poets write _____.

Margo buys _____.

Students enjoy _____.

Name _____ Date _____

Helping Verbs

Sometimes a main verb is lazy. It needs a helper to show action and time. A **helping verb** comes before the main verb in a sentence. The main verb and its helpers form a **verb phrase.** Some common helping verbs are *am, is, are, was, were, will, must, can, may, have,* and *do.*

┌── helping ──┐ ┌─ main ─┐
│   verbs   │ │ verb │
Sheila **should have called.**
└────── verb phrase ──────┘

The subject and verb phrase form the main idea of the sentence. The main idea may include a direct object.

Carlo	can fix	cars

Write a helping verb on the line to complete each sentence. Then write the first and last sentences on the graphic organizers below.

1. Lightning _____ flashing.

2. I _____ get a haircut.

3. They _____ painting fences.

4. We _____ fly biplanes.

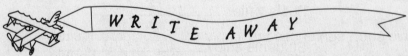

WRITE AWAY

On another sheet of paper, write six short sentences that contain helping verbs. Include direct objects in some of your sentences. Then draw six graphic organizers and write your sentences in the organizers. Be sure to write each part in the correct place.

Core Skills Writing 5, SV 9781419034152

Linking Verbs

What do you think a **linking verb** does? If you said that it links, you're right. A linking verb links the subject to a noun or an adjective in the complete predicate. Some linking verbs are *is, are, was, were, am,* and *been*. Some linking verbs can also be action verbs. These include *feel, look, seem, smell,* and *taste*.

If the verb links the subject to a noun or pronoun, that noun or pronoun is called a **predicate nominative.** If the verb links the subject to an adjective, that adjective is called a **predicate adjective.**

They **are soldiers.** ⟵ (predicate nominative)
We **feel sick.** ⟵ (predicate adjective)

The predicate nominative and predicate adjective are part of the main idea of the sentence. When you write them in a graphic organizer, they go in the same place as the direct object. But the short bar leans back toward the subject. This leaning bar shows that the predicate nominative or predicate adjective is linked to the subject.

They	are \ soldiers		We	feel \ sick

✎ **Write a predicate nominative or predicate adjective to complete each sentence. Then write the sentence on the graphic organizer.**

1. Kara looks _____.

2. Eddie is _____.

3. That smells _____.

On another sheet of paper, write five short sentences that contain linking verbs. Include a predicate nominative or predicate adjective in each sentence. Then draw five graphic organizers and write your sentences in the organizers.

Name _____ Date _____

Review: The Main Idea of a Sentence

The main idea of a sentence is the most important part of the sentence. It tells the most important information in the sentence.

- The main idea may include only a simple subject and a simple predicate.
  Lori laughed.

- The main idea may include a simple subject, a simple predicate, and a direct object.
  Dexter drew pictures.

- The main idea may include a subject, a linking verb, and a linked noun or adjective.
  They are astronauts.   Sadie seems sad.

Remember where each part of the sentence belongs in the graphic organizer.

| subject | verb | object | | subject | verb | predicate adjective or predicate nominative |

Write a sentence that will fit each graphic organizer below. Then write your sentence on the line.

1. _____|_____

   _____

2. _____|_____|_____

   _____

3. _____|_____|_____

   _____

4. _____|_____

   _____

Adding Details to Sentences

The main idea tells the most important part of a sentence. But you may want to include more information. You can add **details.** Details tell more about the main idea. Details can tell whose, which, when, where, and how. Details make your sentence more interesting.

The silly duck took **my mustard** sandwich.

You can see the main idea of the sentence in the graphic organizer below. All the parts of the main idea go above the main idea line. All the details go below the line. *The, silly, my,* and *mustard* are adjectives that modify nouns in the sentence. Place the adjectives under the words they modify.

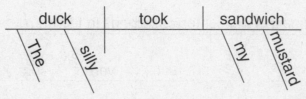

Write details on the lines to complete each sentence. Then get a copy of the Sentence Graphic Organizers on page 120. Write each sentence on one of the organizers. Add lines on the organizer if necessary.

1. The _____ woman sings.

2. A _____ dog chased a _____ cat.

3. The _____ boat hit the _____ rocks.

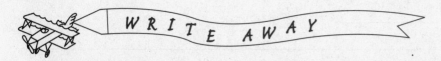

Write details on the lines to complete each sentence. Then, on another sheet of paper, draw two graphic organizers and write your sentences in the organizers. Be sure to write each part in the correct place.

The _____ monkey ate a _____ banana.

A _____ horse pulled a _____ wagon.

Expanding Sentences with Adjectives

What's the difference between a green glass and a yellow glass? A couple of adjectives. **Adjectives** modify nouns and pronouns. Adjectives give details that help us tell one thing from another. With adjectives, we know the difference between a sunny sky and a stormy sky. Adjectives add spice to writing. But as with most spices, you don't want to add too many adjectives.

- Look for sentences that do not give your ideas clearly.
- Think of adjectives that give a more exact picture.

The full moon crossed **the dark** sky.

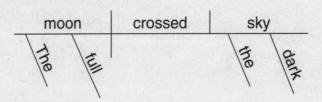

🖝 **Add adjectives to expand each sentence. Write your new sentence on the line.**

1. Snakes slither.

_____

2. Bands play music.

_____

3. The house had spiders.

_____

4. The woman carried a cane.

_____

On another sheet of paper, write adjectives that tell about colors. See how many adjectives you can write.

Name _____ Date _____

Appealing to the Reader's Senses

Writing a good description is a special skill. You can make your reader see, smell, taste, hear, or feel just as you do. To be a good descriptive writer, you must appeal to the reader's senses. Many adjectives appeal to these senses. Choose adjectives carefully to match your purpose and voice.

- **sight:** black, square, large, near
- **touch:** fuzzy, rough, cold, hot
- **hearing:** noisy, quiet, squeaky
- **smell:** smoky, dusty, rotten
- **taste:** sour, salty, sweet

Choose adjectives that you could use to describe each object. Write the adjectives on the line.

1. a strawberry _____

2. an ice-cream cone _____

3. a snake _____

4. a bowl of soup _____

5. the last seconds in a basketball game _____

WRITE AWAY

Write adjectives that tell about each sense. How many adjectives can you write for each sense?

sight _____

touch _____

hearing _____

smell _____

taste _____

Unit 2: Building Sentences
Core Skills Writing 5, SV 9781419034152

Name _____ Date _____

Expanding Sentences with Adverbs

The difference between doing something and doing something well is just an adverb. Adverbs modify verbs, adjectives, or other adverbs. Most adverbs tell how, when, or where. Many adverbs end in *ly*.

The muskrat **slowly** waddled.   (how)
I saw them **yesterday.**   (when)
The lightning struck **here.**   (where)

Adverbs are details that go under the main idea line in a graphic organizer. Write adverbs under the words they modify.

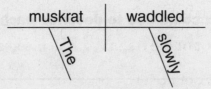

Write an adverb to expand each sentence. Then get a copy of the Sentence Graphic Organizers on page 120. Write each sentence on one of the organizers. Add lines on the organizer if necessary.

1. The lion roared _____.

2. I saw that movie _____.

3. A ball rolled _____.

4. The box arrived _____.

5. A hawk circled _____.

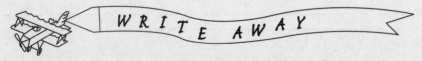

Write five adverbs that fit each group.

tell how: _____

tell when: _____

tell where: _____

Name _____ Date _____

Negatives

A **negative** is a word that means "no" or "not." Many negatives are adverbs or adjectives. Some negatives are nouns or pronouns.

- *Never* and *not* are adverbs.
- *Nobody* is a pronoun.
- *No* can be a noun, an adjective, or an adverb.
- *Nothing* and *nowhere* can be adverbs or nouns.
- *None* can be a pronoun or an adverb.
- The negative *not* is often used in contractions.

    Nobody wants the rotten eggs.
    Ned **never** needs needles.
    She **didn't** buy the book.

Do not use two negatives, or a **double negative,** in the same sentence.

    The baseball player **didn't** get **no** hits.   (incorrect)
    The baseball player **didn't** get **any** hits.   (correct)
    The baseball player got **no** hits.   (correct)

Rewrite each sentence. Be sure not to use double negatives.

1. Willie didn't want no books.

_____

2. Willie doesn't want no facts clogging his brain.

_____

3. Willie never keeps newspapers nowhere.

_____

4. No smart people are never welcome at Willie's house.

_____

Review: Modifiers

You can add details to a sentence by using modifiers such as adjectives and adverbs.

- An adjective modifies a noun or a pronoun. **black** bear
- An adverb modifies a verb, an adjective, or another adverb.

  walking **slowly**   **really** cold   **very** carefully

Modifiers are written under the main idea line in a graphic organizer. Write modifiers under the words they modify.

Write a sentence that will fit each graphic organizer below. Then write your sentence on the line.

1.

_____

2.

_____

3.

_____

4.

_____

Clauses and Phrases

A **clause** is a group of related words that includes a subject and a predicate. An **independent clause** tells a complete thought. It may stand alone as a sentence. The main idea of a sentence forms an independent clause.

Lions roar.

A **phrase** is a group of words that does not have a subject or a predicate. Phrases are not complete sentences. They do not tell a complete thought.

in the jungle

You can also put an independent clause and a phrase together.

Lions roar in the jungle.

Circle the clause in each sentence. Draw a line under the phrase.

1. Whales swim in the ocean.

2. Bats fly in the evening.

3. Tessa found the box by the door.

4. The machine came with instructions.

5. At the beach the seagulls squawk.

6. He will fix the toaster for ten dollars.

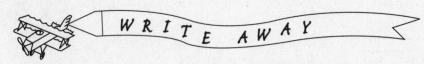

W R I T E   A W A Y

On another sheet of paper, write seven short clauses and seven short phrases. Then cut them out. Mix and match the clauses and phrases. Can you make funny sentences?

Clauses and Phrases, page 2

In a graphic organizer, a phrase goes under the independent clause. The phrase "in the jungle" tells where, so it is an adverb. It is written under the predicate. Study the special lines the phrase is written on.

Lions | roar
in jungle
the

Add a clause or a phrase to complete each sentence. Then write the first sentence on the graphic organizer. On another sheet of paper, draw graphic organizers for sentences 2.–5. Write each sentence on its organizer. Drawing an organizer is like working a puzzle.

1. _____ at the beach.

2. Horses gallop _____.

3. Squirrels live _____.

4. _____ in the desert.

5. _____ geese honk.

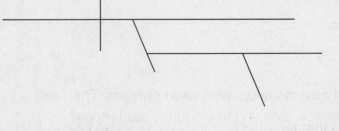

Remember adjectives and adverbs? They can be in sentences with phrases. On another sheet of paper, draw a graphic organizer for the sentence below. Write the sentence on the organizer.

Green frogs paddle lazily through the lily pads.

Unit 2: Building Sentences
Core Skills Writing 5, SV 9781419034152

Expanding Sentences with Prepositional Phrases

Many phrases you write will be **prepositional phrases.** Prepositional phrases are made up of a preposition, its object, and any other words.

- Remember, a preposition shows the relation of a noun or pronoun to another word in a sentence.
- Some prepositions are *of, at, in, on, to, up,* and *from.*
- The noun or pronoun that follows the preposition is called the **object of the preposition.**
- Prepositional phrases can tell where, when, whose, why, how, or which.

   I found a rare coin **in the parking lot.**   (where)
   She made the meal **in a hurry.**   (how)
   A man **in a wheelchair** opened the door.   (which)

Add a phrase to each sentence. Your phrase should tell where, when, whose, why, how, or which.

1. The smelly shoes belonged _____.

2. They did their exercises _____.

3. Uncle Hugo will leave _____.

4. Emma went _____.

5. Aunt Twilly made lunch _____.

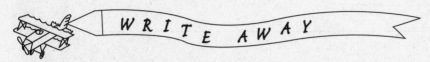

W R I T E   A W A Y

On another sheet of paper, write ten phrases that tell where your missing house key could be hidden.   (behind the sofa)

Expanding Sentences with Prepositional Phrases, page 2

Prepositional phrases can tell where, when, whose, why, or how. These kinds of prepositional phrases usually modify the predicate. On a graphic organizer, each would be written under the predicate.

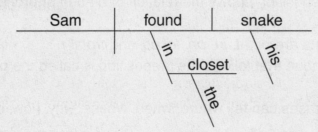

Prepositional phrases can also be used to tell which. This kind of prepositional phrase usually modifies the subject. On a graphic organizer, the phrase would be written under the subject.

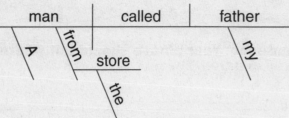

✍ **Write a prepositional phrase to complete each sentence. Look at the word in parentheses to tell what kind of prepositional phrase to write.**

1. Jarrell traveled _____. (where)

2. I mailed the package _____. (when)

3. The new car belonged _____. (whose)

4. Tena studied the problems _____. (why)

5. Matt moved a mongoose _____. (how)

6. The paper _____ was torn. (which)

On another sheet of paper, draw a graphic organizer for each of the sentences above. Write the sentence on the graphic organizer.

Name _____ Date _____

Expanding Sentences with Coordinate Conjunctions

Remember that a **conjunction** is a connective. It joins words or groups of words. **Coordinate conjunctions** are one important kind of conjunction. A coordinate conjunction joins two words, two phrases, or two clauses of equal rank. Some coordinate conjunctions are *and, or, but, yet,* and *still.*

Carlo **and** his dog   (*and* joins two nouns)
safe **yet** fun   (*yet* joins two adjectives)
in the garage **or** on the toaster   (*or* joins two prepositional phrases)

You can expand a sentence by using coordinate conjunctions. You can write compound subjects, compound predicates, compound modifiers, and compound sentences. Conjunctions are quite useful in writing.

Write sentences using coordinate conjunctions. Use a coordinate conjunction to join the kinds of words named in parentheses.

1. (verbs) _____

2. (adjectives) _____

3. (nouns) _____

4. (prepositional phrases) _____

_____

5. (independent clauses) _____

_____

Try to count the number of times you say or write the word *and* every day. On another sheet of paper, write a few sentences about living in a world without coordinate conjunctions.

Name _____ Date _____

Compound Subjects

A **compound subject** has two or more simple subjects. The subjects are joined by a coordinate conjunction.

Carmelo *and* **Tiara** sing in the choir.
Sid *or* **Cynthia** saved the sardines.

When you write a compound subject in a graphic organizer, you add the conjunction on a dotted line. The dotted line connects the two subjects.

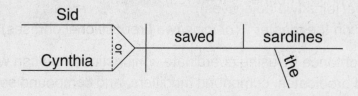

✎ **Write a compound subject to complete each sentence. Write the last sentence on the graphic organizer.**

1. _____ heard a strange noise.

2. _____ probably made the noise.

3. _____ rattled in the attic.

4. Then _____ rang the doorbell.

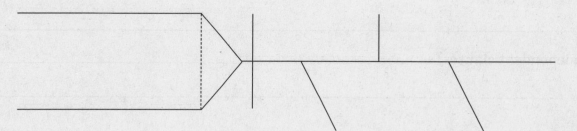

On another sheet of paper, write seven compound subjects and seven predicates. Cut them out. Mix and match the compound subjects and the predicates. Can you make silly sentences? Draw a graphic organizer for one of your sentences and write your sentence on it.

Name _____ Date _____

Compound Predicates

A **compound predicate** has two or more simple predicates. The predicates are joined by a coordinate conjunction.

The football players **ran** *and* **tackled.**
You must **work** *or* **leave.**
Elena **hopped, skipped,** *and* **tumbled.**

When you write a compound predicate in a graphic organizer, you add the conjunction on a dotted line. The dotted line connects the two predicates.

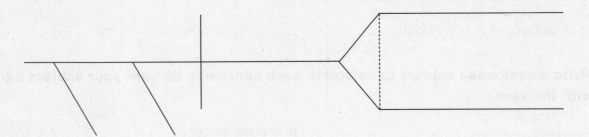

✎ **Write a compound predicate to complete each sentence. Write the last sentence on the graphic organizer.**

1. Basketball players _____.

2. They might _____.

3. The lightning _____.

4. The howling wind _____.

On another sheet of paper, write six compound subjects and six compound predicates. Cut them out. Mix and match the compound subjects and the compound predicates. Are your sentences interesting? Draw a graphic organizer for one of your sentences and write your sentence on it.

Core Skills Writing 5, SV 9781419034152

Name _____ Date _____

Agreement of Verbs and Compound Subjects

The subject of a sentence must agree in number with the verb.

- A singular subject must have a singular verb.
- A plural subject must have a plural verb.

A compound subject that uses *and* is a plural subject. It requires a plural verb.

   Camping *and* swimming **are** fun.

A compound subject that uses *or* can be plural or singular. The verb agrees with the part of the compound subject closer to the verb.

   An orange *or* a banana **is** a good choice.   (singular)
   Carrots *or* an apple **is** a healthy snack.   (singular)
   An apple *or* carrots **are** a healthy snack.   (plural)

Write *is* or *are* to complete each sentence. Be sure your verb agrees with the subject.

1. Those girls or Chad _____ wrong.

2. Math and history _____ hard subjects.

3. Donkeys or bats _____ in the attic.

4. A box of mice or a box of balls _____ in the hall.

Write a compound subject to complete each sentence. Be sure your subject agrees with the verb.

5. _____ or _____ make me sneeze.

6. _____ or a _____ is in the letter.

7. _____ or _____ make a good sandwich.

On another sheet of paper, write five sentences. Each sentence should have a compound subject and a compound predicate. Be sure your verbs agree with your compound subject. Both verbs will be either singular or plural.

Subordinate Conjunctions

Subordinate conjunctions are another important kind of conjunction. A subordinate conjunction joins two clauses of unequal rank. A subordinate conjunction joins a **dependent clause** to an independent clause. The independent clause has a higher rank than the dependent clause. The main idea of the sentence goes in the independent clause. Some subordinate conjunctions are *as, because, before, since, when, where,* and *that.*

The weather was hot **before the rain fell.** ⟵ subordinate clause

I was late **because my dog ate my clock.** ⟵ subordinate clause

Write a dependent clause to complete each sentence. Use the subordinate conjunction in the sentence.

1. We got lost because _____.

2. We had not been hiking since _____

3. We were rescued before _____

4. We were so scared that _____

5. We may go hiking again when _____

W R I T E   A W A Y

Write five sentences that begin like the sentence below.

I like writing because _____.

_____

_____

_____

_____

_____

Name _____ Date _____

Review: Connectives

Conjunctions and prepositions are connectives. Connectives join parts of a sentence.

- A coordinate conjunction connects words or groups of words of equal rank. Some coordinate conjunctions are *and, or, but,* and *yet.*
- A subordinate conjunction joins two clauses of unequal rank. Some subordinate conjunctions are *because, before,* and *that.*
- A preposition shows the relation of a noun or pronoun to another word in a sentence. Some prepositions are *of, at, in, on, to, up, by,* and *from.*
- The preposition, its object, and any other words make up a prepositional phrase.

A graphic organizer shows the role of each connective in the sentence.

Jill **and** Jack went **down** the track.

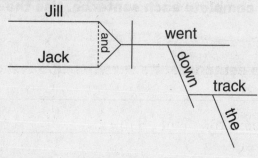

Write a sentence that will fit each graphic organizer below. Then write your sentence on the line. You can add lines to the graphic organizer if necessary.

1. _____

_____

2. _____

Kinds of Sentences

There are four basic kinds of sentences: declarative, interrogative, imperative, and exclamatory.

- Use a **declarative sentence** to make a statement. You give information with this kind of sentence.
- Begin a declarative sentence with a capital letter. End it with a **period (.)**.

   Venus is a planet.   The moon has no atmosphere.

- Use an **interrogative sentence** to ask a question. You get information with this kind of sentence.
- Begin an interrogative sentence with a capital letter. End it with a **question mark (?)**.

   Where are we going?   Will we be there soon?

👈 **Follow the directions to write sentences. Be sure to begin and end each sentence correctly.**

1. Write a declarative sentence about the planet Saturn.

   _____

2. Write an interrogative sentence about the planet Saturn.

   _____

3. Write a declarative sentence about your state.

   _____

4. Write an interrogative sentence about your state.

   _____

5. Write an interrogative sentence about declarative sentences.

   _____

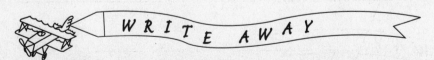

On another sheet of paper, write six interrogative sentences. Then write six declarative sentences to answer your questions.

Kinds of Sentences, page 2

There are four basic kinds of sentences: declarative, interrogative, imperative, and exclamatory.

- Use an **imperative sentence** to make a request or to give a command. You use this kind of sentence to make people do something.
- Begin an imperative sentence with a capital letter. End it with a period or an **exclamation mark (!)**.
- The subject of an imperative sentence is the person to whom the request or command is given (*you*). The subject usually does not appear in the sentence. It is called an **understood subject.**

    (You) Please hand in your project.   (You) Get your feet off the sofa!

- Use an **exclamatory sentence** to show excitement or strong feeling. You use this kind of sentence when you are excited.
- Begin an exclamatory sentence with a capital letter. End it with an exclamation mark.

    A mudslide is heading this way!   I love exclamatory sentences!

Follow the directions to write sentences. Be sure to begin and end each sentence correctly.

1. Write an imperative sentence about setting the table.

_____

2. Write an exclamatory sentence about a tornado.

_____

3. Write an imperative sentence about a package.

_____

4. Write an exclamatory sentence about a car wreck.

_____

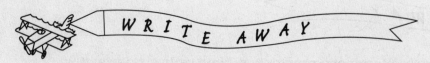

On another sheet of paper, write six imperative sentences that give a command. Then write six exclamatory sentences that respond to the commands.

End Punctuation

Be sure to use the correct punctuation at the end of your sentences.

- Use a **period (.)** at the end of a declarative sentence.
- Use a **question mark (?)** at the end of an interrogative sentence.
- Use a period or an **exclamation mark (!)** at the end of an imperative sentence.
- Use an exclamation mark at the end of an exclamatory sentence.

My pet hamster is missing.   Has anyone seen it?
Help us search for it.   It's in the microwave!

Follow the directions to write sentences. Then tell what kind each sentence is.

1. Write a sentence that ends with a period.

_____

2. Write a sentence that ends with a question mark.

_____

3. Write a sentence that ends with an exclamation mark.

_____

4. Write a sentence that ends with a question mark.

_____

5. Write a sentence that ends with an exclamation mark.

_____

6. Write a sentence that ends with a period.

_____

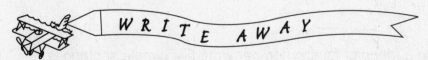

W R I T E   A W A Y

Think about the sentences you write. Which end punctuation mark do you use most often? On another sheet of paper, tell which mark you use most and why.

Name _____   Date _____

Simple, Compound, and Complex Sentences

- A **simple sentence** is a complete sentence. It contains only one complete thought.

    Marco did his homework.

- A **compound sentence** has two or more simple sentences. It has two or more complete thoughts.

- A compound sentence is joined by a coordinate conjunction such as *and, or,* or *but.* A **comma (,)** is used before a conjunction to join two simple sentences.

    Marco did his homework, **and** then his dog ate it.

- A **complex sentence** contains one independent clause and one or more dependent clauses.

    The dog ate the homework because Marco forgot to feed it.

Rewrite each simple sentence to make it a compound or complex sentence.

1. Eva needed help.

   _____

2. Terrell pulled the yellow wagon.

   _____

3. The clouds turned gray.

   _____

4. Karla was nervous.

   _____

Write five simple sentences. Have a friend or family member write five simple sentences, too. Then exchange sentences. Rewrite each other's simple sentences to make them compound sentences.

Using Commas

Commas have many uses in sentences.

- Use a **comma** before the word *and, but,* or *or* when two sentences are joined in a compound sentence.

    The owl hooted, **and** the long night began.

- Use commas to separate three or more words in a **series**.

    The hiker carried **a bedroll, some food, and a flashlight.**

- Use a comma to separate an introductory word or name from the rest of the sentence.

    Jesse, where have you been?   **Yes,** we have been waiting for you.

Complete each compound sentence by adding a second sentence. Be sure to add a comma and a conjunction.

1. The owl flew away _____.

2. Lightning flashed in the dark sky _____.

3. The storm had arrived _____.

Complete each sentence by adding a series of three or more words. Be sure to add commas and a conjunction.

4. The wild dogs _____.

5. The new movie was _____.

6. _____ were in the cold basement.

Complete each sentence by adding an introductory name or word. Be sure to add a comma.

7. _____ we will help them tomorrow.

8. _____ why is this trash in the middle of the floor?

Combining Sentences

Using too many short sentences in your writing is boring. You can make your writing more interesting by combining sentences.

- Sentences that have ideas that go together can be combined.
- Join the sentences with a coordinate conjunction and a comma.

Be sure the conjunction makes the meaning of the combined sentences clear. *And* shows addition, *but* shows difference, and *or* shows choice.

The rocket may land on the planet. The rocket may stay in orbit.
The rocket may land on the planet, **or** it may stay in orbit.

Write a second sentence that is related to the first sentence. Then join the two sentences. Use the conjunction in ( ) to join the sentences. Make sure your sentence agrees with the meaning of the conjunction.

1. The landing on the strange planet was rough.   (but)

Second sentence: _____

Combined sentence: _____

_____

2. Captain Spaceley stuck his head out a porthole.   (and)

Second sentence: _____

Combined sentence: _____

_____

3. Captain Spaceley did not look carefully.   (or)

Second sentence: _____

Combined sentence: _____

_____

4. A meteor flew past his head.   (but)

Second sentence: _____

Combined sentence: _____

_____

Core Skills Writing 5, SV 9781419034152

Combining Sentences with the Same Subject or Predicate

A good writer may choose to combine two or more sentences that have the same subject or predicate. The conjunctions *and, or,* and *but* are often used to combine sentence parts.

- When two sentences have the same predicate, the subjects can be combined. When you combine subjects, be sure you use the correct form of the verb.

    Theseus was angry. King Minos was angry.
    Theseus *and* King Minos were angry.

- When two sentences have the same subject, the predicates can be combined.

    Theseus found the ring. Theseus returned it.
    Theseus **found the ring *and* returned it.**

➤ **Rewrite this paragraph. Combine sentences with the same subjects or predicates to make it more interesting to read. Use another sheet of paper.**

Each year, King Minos demanded a human sacrifice from the people of Athens. Seven boys would enter the Labyrinth. Seven girls would enter the Labyrinth. The Labyrinth was the home of the Minotaur. The Minotaur was half man. The Minotaur was half beast. The boys were devoured by the Minotaur. The girls were devoured by the Minotaur. Finally, Theseus found the Minotaur in the Labyrinth. Theseus killed the Minotaur in the Labyrinth.

WRITE AWAY

Here's something just for fun. On another sheet of paper, write the story of the fight between Theseus and the Minotaur. Write your story in short sentences. Then read your story to find sentences with subjects or predicates that you can combine. Rewrite the paragraph using the new combined sentences.

Name _____ Date _____

Review: Working with Sentences

You can make your writing better by using different kinds of sentences. You can make your writing livelier by joining sentences or parts of sentences.

Follow the directions to write sentences. Be sure to begin and end each sentence correctly.

1. Write a simple interrogative sentence about a baseball game.

_____

_____

2. Write a compound declarative sentence about your favorite hobby.

_____

3. Write a simple exclamatory sentence about the winter.

_____

4. Write a compound imperative sentence about cleaning the house.

_____

5. Form a compound sentence by writing a second sentence. Be sure to add a comma and a conjunction.

The baby bird fell from the nest _____.

6. Write a complex sentence that uses the subordinate conjunction *because*.

_____

_____

7. Combine the two short sentences into one longer sentence.

He started down the path. He stopped when he heard a noise.

_____

_____

Active and Passive Verbs

Strong verbs make writing livelier and more active. They keep your reader interested. Try this. Write a sentence and read it aloud. How does it sound? Does it make you fall asleep? Maybe you need stronger verbs. Let's test. What do you think of this sentence?

The winter weather **was** cold.

This sentence is not very exciting. The verb *was* is rather weak. *Was* is a **passive verb**. All of the *be* verbs (*is, are, was, were, am, be, been, being*) are passive. The sentence needs an **active verb**.

The winter cold **froze** us.

Froze is an active verb. The reader can "see" the action in his or her head and becomes more interested. So, to make your writing more interesting, use active verbs as much as possible.

Rewrite each sentence. Change the passive verbs to active verbs. You may have to change the way the sentence is written.

1. Marcy was sad.

_____

2. The weather was nice.

_____

3. The painting was done by Yoko.

_____

4. The contest was won by the Gophers.

_____

5. We were glad that the test was over.

_____

Begin a list of every active verb you can think of. In your spare time, add more active verbs to your list. Use this list to help you in your writing.

Core Skills Writing 5, SV 9781419034152

Name _____ Date _____

Verb Tense

Tense means "time." So **verb tense** tells the time a verb action is happening.

- Use a **present tense verb** to tell what is happening now.
- Use a **past tense verb** to tell what happened in the past.
- Use a **future tense verb** to tell what will happen in the future.

He **hops** now.   He **hopped** yesterday.   He **will hop** tomorrow.
(present tense)   (past tense)   (future tense)

If you use the wrong verb tense in your writing, your reader will be lost. Be sure to use the same verb tense throughout your piece of writing.

Write a verb to complete each sentence. Use clues in the sentence to write the correct verb tense.

1. Sara _____ in a play yesterday.

2. She _____ in the same play tomorrow.

3. Reese _____ his new job today.

4. He _____ the morning shift next week.

5. Now the wind _____.

6. Later today, it _____ again.

7. Yesterday, the wind _____ all day.

8. I hope the wind _____ soon.

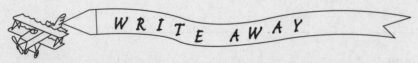

W R I T E   A W A Y

Write a list of twelve verbs. Then make a chart with three columns. At the top of one column, write *present tense*. At the top of the second column, write *past tense*. At the top of the third column, write *future tense*. Write your twelve verbs in the correct place in the chart. Complete the chart by writing the correct tense of each verb in the columns.

Writing Descriptive Sentences

When you write a descriptive sentence, you want to give the reader many details. Use specific details that tell who, what, when, where, and how. Your descriptive sentence should let the reader "see" the scene in his or her mind. The following sentence tells about the object, but the reader cannot "see" the scene.

Mount Rushmore is great and wonderful.

This sentence needs more specific adjectives than "great" and "wonderful." These adjectives only tell what the writer thinks about the object. They don't really describe the object. Here's a better descriptive sentence.

The four giant granite faces of Mount Rushmore gaze across the rolling countryside.

Good descriptive sentences use strong verbs and specific adjectives and adverbs.

Rewrite each sentence to make it more descriptive. Use strong verbs and specific adjectives or adverbs.

1. The night was dark.

_____

2. The music was nice.

_____

3. The fireworks were pretty.

_____

4. The desert was dry.

_____

5. The actor was handsome.

_____

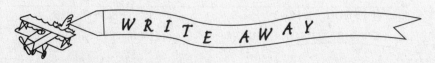

WRITE AWAY

What is your favorite food? On another sheet of paper, write four descriptive sentences about it. Use strong verbs and specific adjectives or adverbs.

Writing Descriptive Sentences, page 2

Good description creates a mental picture for your readers. How do you create a mental picture? You use details. Adjectives are good for details. Adjectives can tell color, size, smell, feeling, and all the good senses. You want your words to control what your readers "see" in their minds. You must appeal to their senses. Think about your word choices. That's what good writers do.

The sweet juice of the red watermelon made my tongue tingle.

☛ **You want to describe rain for someone. Write five adjectives for each sense. Remember to think about your choices.**

Sight: _____

Smell: _____

Touch: _____

Sound: _____

Taste: _____

☛ **Choose the best adjective for each sense from your lists above. Use the five best adjectives to write a descriptive paragraph about rain. Use another sheet of paper. Be sure to create a mental picture for your reader. Don't just write sentences listing the adjectives.**

Best adjectives: _____

_____

_____

_____

_____

WRITE AWAY

Find a colorful picture or painting that you like. Write five sentences to describe it.

Writing Descriptive Sentences, page 3

Strong adjectives are good for creating mental pictures. Adverbs are good, too. But strong verbs are even better.

The explosion **blasted** the building to bits.

Write five active verbs that mean the same as the words given. Write only verbs. Do not use adverbs.

1. eat _____

2. move quickly _____

3. find _____

4. move unsteadily _____

5. see _____

Revise each sentence. Use a strong verb and strong adjectives. Make your writing clear and direct.

6. The man who was about 80 years old moved unsteadily to the envelope that was red.

_____

7. The colorful dogs that were running around the park were making barking sounds.

_____

8. The sunset was beautiful.

_____

WRITE AWAY

On another sheet of paper, rewrite the sentence below five times. Replace the verb with a stronger verb in each sentence.

Carli moved through the cold, dark tunnel.

Name _____ Date _____

Using Figurative Language

Writers sometimes use **figurative language** to compare unlike things. The words in figurative language don't really mean what they say. If a man is very hungry, he might say he could eat a horse. He doesn't really mean it, though. He is using figurative language.

- A **simile** compares two things by using *like* or *as.*

  The storm swept over the plains **like a giant mop.**
  He was as busy **as a beaver.**

Figurative language is fun for creating mental pictures.

  His truck was as big **as a house.**

Complete each simile.

1. The thick, green grass was like _____.

2. Life is sometimes like _____.

3. The cat was as friendly as _____.

4. The blooming flowers were like _____.

5. The dog ran like _____.

6. The rain on the roof sounded like _____.

W R I T E   A W A Y

Rewrite each sentence below. State the same idea but use a simile.

Kayla was very warm.

_____

The cheetah ran quickly.

_____

Unit 2: Building Sentences
Core Skills Writing 5, SV 9781419034152

Name _____ Date _____

Using Figurative Language, page 2

When you use figurative language, you can create strong pictures in your reader's mind. You can create vivid word pictures by comparing two things that are not usually thought to be alike.

- **Personification** makes nonhuman things seem human. Objects, ideas, places, or animals may be given human qualities.

  Even the **leaves** of the trees **laughed** at me.
  The **waves danced** along the shoreline.
  The **sad rattlesnake** talked to his **best friend**, the **rhyming rat**.

Rewrite each sentence but do not use personification.

1. The mist crept silently into the village.

_____

2. The tree fought the wind with its branches.

_____

3. The friendly hills seemed to welcome us home.

_____

Rewrite each sentence but use personification to make it more interesting.

4. It was sunny out.

_____

5. The tree branches were moving in the wind.

_____

On another sheet of paper, write sentences that personify these things.

    a toaster   a turtle   a trash can

Sentence Beginnings

Sentence variety makes your writing more interesting. Sentences that all begin the same way are boring. There's an old saying that "variety is the spice of life." Well, variety is the spice of writing, too. Let's look at some ways to spice up your writing.

- You can begin a sentence with an adjective.

   Beautiful were the voices in the choir.

- You can begin a sentence with an adverb.

   Quickly the firefighter put out the flame.

- You can begin a sentence with a preposition.

   Behind the bush the frightened dog hid.

⬧ **Follow the directions to write sentences. Be sure to begin and end each sentence correctly.**

1. Write a sentence about trees that begins with an adjective.

   _____

2. Write a sentence about a hawk that begins with a preposition.

   _____

3. Write a sentence about an explorer that begins with a preposition.

   _____

4. Write a sentence about a flying duck that begins with an adverb.

   _____

W R I T E   A W A Y

Write a sentence that has at least eight words. Then think of all the different ways you can say the same thing. How many different ways can you begin the sentence? On another sheet of paper, write at least three versions of your sentence.

Original sentence: _____

Sentence Lengths

You can also get variety by changing the lengths of the sentences you write.

- Short sentences clearly tell the main idea.

    My **rat is missing.**

- Short sentences can present strong actions.

    A **skier flew** down the hillside.

- Longer sentences help to explain details better.

- Compound sentences let you tell about two related ideas.

    A **storm rumbled** across the valley, **and Mario quickly carried firewood** to the small cabin.

✎ Follow the directions to write sentences. Be sure to begin and end each sentence correctly.

1. Write a short sentence that shows a main idea clearly.

_____

2. Write a short sentence that shows a strong action.

_____

3. Write a longer sentence with several details.

_____

4. Write a longer compound sentence about two related ideas.

_____

_____

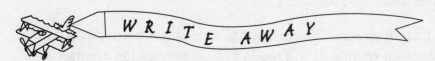

On another sheet of paper, practice writing the same idea in sentences of different lengths. Do the shorter or longer sentences help you express yourself better?

Sentence Errors: Fragments

A good sentence expresses a complete idea. It has a subject and a predicate, and it uses correct punctuation. But sentence errors can make your writing unclear and confusing. You need to check your writing to be sure you do not have sentence errors.

One common error is the **sentence fragment.** A sentence fragment is only a part of a sentence. It is not a complete sentence, and it does not tell a complete thought. You should remove fragments from your writing.

Had a good time at the movie.   (fragment—no subject)
Tonya and some of the other girls.   (fragment—no predicate)
At the end of the year.   (fragment—prepositional phrases)
I learned about sentence fragments today.   (complete sentence)

Rewrite each fragment to make it a complete sentence. If the group of words is a complete sentence already, write *not a fragment*.

1. Almost time for the TV show.

_____

2. We fly through the treetops.

_____

3. Buried treasure at the beach.

_____

4. Caught some fish in the pond.

_____

5. Many kinds of turtles in the water.

_____

6. The driver in the car and another man on a bike.

_____

_____

Sentence Errors: Run-on Sentences

Another common error is the **run-on sentence.** A run-on sentence can happen in two ways.

- A run-on can happen when you join two complete sentences without any punctuation. This error is also known as a **fused sentence.**
- To fix a run-on like this, join the two sentences with a comma and a coordinate conjunction.
- You can also use a period and write the run-on sentence as two separate sentences.
- You can also join the two sentences with a subordinate conjunction. You must make one idea more important than the other idea.

> We started early we still arrived late.   (run-on)
> We started early, **but** we still arrived late.   (fixed)
> We started early. We still arrived late.   (fixed)
> **Though** we started early, we still arrived late.   (fixed)

 Correct each run-on sentence. Write the new sentence or sentences on the line.

1. I had a turtle once its name was Turk E. Turtle.

_____

2. A box turtle is a reptile it lives in fields and forests.

_____

3. Painted turtles eat worms and insects the musk turtle finds food in ponds and streams.

_____

_____

4. This game is for small groups up to four people may play.

_____

5. The player with the most points wins the winner receives no prize.

_____

Name _____ Date _____

Sentence Errors:
Run-on Sentences, page 2

- A run-on can also happen when you join two complete sentences with only a comma. This error is also known as a **comma splice.**
- To fix a run-on like this, use a period and write the run-on sentence as two separate sentences.
- You can also join the two sentences with a comma and a coordinate conjunction.
- You can also join the two sentences with a subordinate conjunction. You must make one idea more important than the other idea.

We spent the summer in Arizona, we had a good time.   (run-on)
We spent the summer in Arizona. We had a good time.   (fixed)
We spent the summer in Arizona, **and** we had a good time.   (fixed)
When we spent the summer in Arizona, we had a good time.   (fixed)

Correct each run-on sentence. Write the new sentence or sentences on the line.

1. The Grand Canyon is in Arizona, it is about 217 miles long.

_____

_____

2. The canyon is about one mile deep, in some places it is 18 miles wide.

_____

_____

3. The Grand Canyon became a national park in 1919, the park covers over a million acres.

_____

_____

4. You can take a burro ride to the canyon floor, you can hike along the South Rim.

_____

_____

Name _____ Date _____

Seeing Your Writing

If you can actually see what you write, you have a much better idea of each part's role in the sentence. You can see the main idea of the sentence and the location of details. Seeing your writing can help you organize it better.

Match each sentence on the left to its graphic organizer on the right. Write the letter of the organizer before the sentence. You may write on the graphic organizers.

_____ **1.** Bats fly in the night.   **A.**

_____ **2.** Chet chewed a chestnut.   **B.**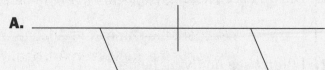

_____ **3.** The mayor called today.   **C.**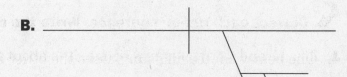

_____ **4.** I met Erica at the mall.   **D.**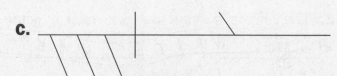

_____ **5.** The black cap on the table is hers.   **E.**

Core Skills Writing 5, SV 9781419034152

Name _____ Date _____

Self-Evaluation: What's Going On?

Think about all you have written so far. What have you learned? Do you think you are a better writer now? Do you know how to write a good sentence? Well, on this page you will get a chance to show all that you have learned.

Each of the following sentences has one or more errors. Study each sentence. Then rewrite each sentence correctly.

1. Did you see those flying bears.

_____

2. I didn't see no flying bears?

_____

3. In a biplane was two bears.

_____

4. One bear was wearing sunglasses the other bear had rollers in her hair.

_____

_____

W R I T E   A W A Y

In this exercise, you should take your time and try to do your best writing. First, on another sheet of paper, write three sentences that tell about something you really like, such as a pet, a hobby, or music. Think of the sentences as your first draft. Get your ideas on paper quickly.

Then revise your sentences. Do the sentences say what you mean? Will your reader understand what you have written? Can the word choice be improved? Think about your sentences for five minutes. Then rewrite each sentence in three different ways. Read each sentence aloud as you are writing it. How does it sound? Is the punctuation correct?

OK, now choose the best version of each sentence. Write the three sentences in final form. Compare your final three sentences to the Self-Evaluation Checklist on page 119. Check each point that agrees with your writing. How good is your writing? On another sheet of paper, write three or four sentences that describe your writing style.

What Is a Paragraph?

A **paragraph** is a group of sentences that tells about one main idea. A paragraph has three parts.

- The **topic sentence** tells the main idea of the paragraph.
- The **detail sentences** tell more about the main idea.
- The **concluding sentence** closes the paragraph. It restates the main idea and summarizes the information in the paragraph.

Read each paragraph below. How well does each paragraph tell about one main idea? Write a few sentences about each paragraph. Tell why it is or is not a good paragraph.

1.   Eels are fish that are shaped like a snake. Most eels are about three feet long. But there are giant eels that grow to be ten feet long. Eels have slimy bodies that may be covered with scales. Eels do not have fins along the sides of their bodies like most fish. They wriggle through the water like a water snake.

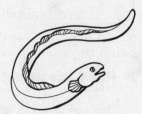

_____

_____

_____

_____

2.   Oceans have currents. Currents are like rivers moving through the ocean waters. I went fishing in a river last summer, but I didn't catch anything. Some currents are warmer than the water around them. Others are colder. When I fell in the river, it was not very cold. Currents move through oceans all over the world.

_____

_____

_____

_____

Name _____ Date _____

What Is in a Paragraph?

A paragraph is a group of sentences about one main idea. The first sentence of the paragraph is **indented,** or moved in five spaces from the left margin. There are usually several sentences in a paragraph. Many paragraphs have five sentences.

When you write a paragraph, you want it to have a certain order. A good paragraph moves from

general —**to**→ specific —**to**→ general.

- The **topic sentence** is general. It names the topic or main idea of the paragraph, but it does not give details.
- The **detail** sentences are specific. They give details about the topic of the paragraph.
- The **concluding sentence** is general. It restates the main idea and sums up the information in the paragraph.

Read the paragraph below. Then write sentences to answer each question.

The nervous system is the system that helps your body respond to the environment. The brain is the main organ of the nervous system. The different body organs send messages through the nerves to the brain. The brain sorts out the messages to tell your body how to react. Without a nervous system, you would not be aware of your surroundings.

1. What is the topic of this paragraph?

_____

_____

2. Write the topic sentence from the paragraph.

_____

_____

3. Write a detail sentence from the paragraph.

_____

_____

4. Write the concluding sentence from the paragraph.

_____

_____

Unit 3: Building Paragraphs
Core Skills Writing 5, SV 9781419034152

Name _____ Date _____

Writing a Topic Sentence

A **topic sentence** tells the topic or main idea of a paragraph. It tells what all the other sentences in the paragraph are about. The topic sentence is usually the first sentence in a paragraph. A topic sentence should have **focus.** Focus means you have narrowed down the topic. For example, you might have the general topic of the Ohio River. You could focus on how goods are transported on the Ohio River.

Language is a set of written or spoken words used to communicate. Language lets parents teach their children. It gives people a way to share what they know and what they do. Language allows people to write their experiences and feelings. These records let people pass on their skills and knowledge.

Read each topic below. Then choose a focus for each topic. Write a topic sentence that you could use to write a paragraph about your topic.

1. Topic: rivers

   Focus: _longest rivers_

   Topic sentence: _The longest river in the world is the Nile River._

2. Topic: sharks

   Focus: _____

   Topic sentence: _____

3. Topic: the Revolutionary War

   Focus: _____

   Topic sentence: _____

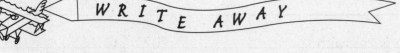
WRITE AWAY

On another sheet of paper, write a paragraph using one of your topic sentences.

Writing Detail Sentences

The body sentences in a paragraph are **detail sentences.** Detail sentences give facts or examples about the topic. Detail sentences help the reader learn more about the topic.

You need to choose your details carefully. Don't put a detail in your paragraph just because you thought of it. A good plan is to list all the details you can think of. Then choose the three details that best support the topic sentence. Include the details in three body sentences.

Language is a set of written or spoken words used to communicate. **Language lets parents teach their children. It gives people a way to share what they know and what they do. Language allows people to write their experiences and feelings.** These records let people pass on their skills and knowledge.

Complete the prewriting steps below. What does Thanksgiving Day make you think of? Write some details. Then narrow your thoughts on Thanksgiving to the given topic sentence.

Topic: Thanksgiving Day

Details about Thanksgiving Day:

_____

_____

Topic sentence (focus): Thanksgiving Day is a time when many families gather and celebrate.

Choose three best details from above for this topic sentence:

_____

_____

_____

Write three detail sentences that support the topic sentence.

_____

_____

_____

Name _____ Date _____

Writing a Concluding Sentence

A **concluding sentence** ends the paragraph. It restates the topic sentence in different words, and it sums up the information in the paragraph. It can also explain what the information means.

Suppose that your paragraph is a sandwich. The two slices of bread hold all the details inside—the lettuce, the tomatoes, the pickle slices. The top slice of bread is the topic sentence. The bottom slice of bread is the concluding sentence. The two slices are similar but not the same, just as the concluding sentence is like the topic sentence but not exactly. Read the paragraph about language again. Notice how the topic sentence and the concluding sentence are similar but not exactly alike. Use the Paragraph Structure Chart on page 124 to organize your ideas.

Language is a set of written or spoken words used to communicate. Language lets parents teach their children. It gives people a way to share what they know and what they do. Language allows people to write their experiences and feelings. **These records let people pass on their skills and knowledge.**

Read the paragraph below. Then write two possible concluding sentences for the paragraph.

Doctors noticed that many sick people had recently had a major life event. Something new had happened to them. A few of them had gained a new home or new job. Others had just been married. The event put them under a lot of stress. Then it was easy for germs to make them sick.

Concluding sentence 1: _____

_____

Concluding sentence 2: _____

_____

Name _____ Date _____

Using Time Order in Paragraphs

A paragraph should have a beginning, a middle, and an end. You can join the parts of the paragraph by using **transition** words, or words that help move from one idea to the next. **Time-order words** are one kind of transition. Some words that show time order are *before*, *after*, *first, next, then,* and *finally*. Read the sample paragraph below. Notice how the time-order words help the sentences flow smoothly.

Do you think you can start a campfire with ice? It can be done. **First,** find a large, thin piece of clear ice. **Then,** shape it by melting it in the palms of your hands. When the ice is ready, it should look like a lens. Both sides should have smooth curves. **Finally,** use the ice to focus the sun's rays onto paper or wood shavings. A fire should start.

Number the sentences in the order the events happened. The topic sentence is numbered for you. Then write the sentences in paragraph form on another sheet of paper. Remember to indent the first sentence.

___1___ The man showed the boy how to start a fire in the wilderness.

_____ Then, when the pile of sticks was burning well, he added some larger sticks and small logs.

_____ Next, he used his magnifying glass to catch the sun's rays and light the moss on fire.

_____ Finally, when the small logs were burning well, he placed a large log on top.

_____ First, the man made a pile of small sticks and dry moss in a circle of rocks.

_____ The man and boy had a good fire to keep them warm that night.

Name _____ Date _____

Prewriting a Paragraph

Anything you want to do well takes practice. This is why writing follows a long process that gives you much time for practice and improvement. **Prewriting** is the first step in the writing process. This is when you think about what you will write. Prewriting is sometimes called **brainstorming.** Prewriting has three main chores.

- think about your topic and audience
- choose details
- organize your ideas

Prewriting is an important skill to practice. Prewriting can take place in the seconds before you write a sentence or in the weeks before a big research project is due. When you prewrite, you work on ideas and words in your mind more than on paper. The Prewriting Survey on pages 113 and 114 can help you with your prewriting chores.

You have an assignment to write a paragraph about your favorite sport. Do some prewriting. Think about what you must write. Fill in the chart below to help you to prewrite.

Main goal of assignment: _____

Nouns I might use: _____

Verbs I might use: _____

Adjectives I might use: _____

Adverbs I might use: _____

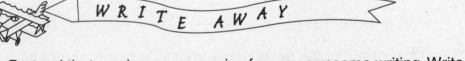

Pretend that you have won a prize for your awesome writing. Write twenty words you might use in your acceptance speech. Use another sheet of paper.

Unit 3: Building Paragraphs
Core Skills Writing 5, SV 9781419034152

Name _____ Date _____

Voice

When you talk to others, they can tell how you feel by listening to your voice. In writing, **voice** is the way a writer "speaks" to the readers. Voice is how your writing sounds. The readers can "hear" how you feel about the topic. Think about the people who might read what you write. With your writing and the care you put into it, you can control what they think and how they feel.

Your voice should fit your topic. To choose your voice for a topic, you must think of your audience.

- You probably wouldn't write cheerfully about sad, hurt people.
- You probably would write cheerfully about people having a party.

Write a sentence to describe the voice in each paragraph. Is the voice serious, funny, happy, sad, or some other emotion?

1. The boy stared at the empty doghouse. Teardrops filled his eyes. Champ would never come home again.

_____

2. Jayla slid safely into home. Her teammates crowded around her. She had won the game!

_____

3. Poverty is a problem in today's world. Many people do not have a place to live. Many do not get enough to eat. Many are sick, and they can't get medical care. We must do something about poverty before it's too late.

_____

4. Parker clicked from one TV channel to the next. Why weren't there any shows for a guy like him? He did not know. But when he heard Farmer Thomas come in the door, he knew he should get back to the barn fast.

_____

Pretend that you made an A on a test. On another sheet of paper, write a short paragraph about your success. Use a happy voice.

Writing Pattern: Main Idea and Details

Writing patterns can help you organize your work. Choosing a pattern in the prewriting step will help you choose a writing form. For example, suppose you want to tell some information about a topic. You would probably choose the main idea and details pattern.

You already know about main idea and details. The main idea is the most important idea. The details tell more about the main idea. Details give a clearer picture of the main idea. When you choose this pattern, the Main Idea and Details Web on page 121 can help you plan your work.

Look at your left thumb. Suppose you have to describe it in an assignment. Use the Main Idea and Details Web on page 121 to write details about your left thumb. Follow the directions to complete the organizer.

1. What is the topic or main idea? Write it in the center oval.

2. Which senses can you use to describe your left thumb? How does it look? What color is it? How does it smell? How does it feel if you touch it? How does it taste? Write one detail in each circle. Draw more circles around the center oval if necessary.

3. What are some words that describe each detail? Write specific adjectives, adverbs, and nouns that you could use to write a paragraph.

Use the Main Idea and Details Web to write a paragraph that gives information about your left thumb. Use another sheet of paper.

Writing Pattern: Summary

Think about the last book you read. If someone asked you about it, what would you say? Would you describe what you ate while you were reading? Would you tell where you sat while you read? You probably would not because you wouldn't want the person to get bored. Instead, you should tell the most important details about the book.

When you **summarize,** you tell the most important information about something. You tell who, what, where, when, why, and how. You might use this writing pattern if you want to give your audience a short description of a book, story, or movie. You may need to summarize information for a research report. Remember to give the most important details so the audience understands the topic, but be brief. You can use the Summary Chart on page 122 to help you plan your work.

Read the paragraph below. Then complete the Summary Chart on page 122. Follow the directions below to complete the chart.

People have long compared animal activity to human behavior. As a result, animals come to stand for certain things. The bee, for example, works continuously, producing honey and helping flowers grow. People, therefore, say that the bee stands for hard work. Another animal, the snail, has come to symbolize slowness because it moves so slowly. The butterfly can symbolize the process of life itself. Butterflies go through four complete changes in their life cycle—from egg to caterpillar to chrysalis to full-grown butterfly. As you can see, animals can be used to illustrate human actions.

1. Write the important details from the paragraph on the left side of the box. Tell who, what, where, when, why, and how. You do not need to write complete sentences.

2. Use the details from the left side of the chart to write a summary. Write complete sentences. Do not include any extra information. Write as few sentences as you can, but be sure to include all the important details.

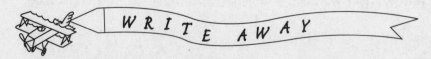

On another sheet of paper, write why you think summarizing is an important writing skill. You can even use the Summary Chart on page 122 to help you plan your work!

Writing Pattern: Sequence of Events

Narratives and how-to directions describe events in order. In both kinds of writing, you would choose a writing pattern that shows the **sequence,** or order, of events. Suppose you want to tell your friend how to feed your pet while you are on vacation. You would write the steps in order. You would use the sequence of events pattern to tell what to do first, next, and last.

Be sure to tell the actions or steps in order. What if you were making lemonade? You would not be very successful if the directions didn't tell you to cut the lemons before you tried to squeeze the juice out.

When you choose this pattern, a sequence chart can help you plan your work. It helps you think about each step. You can plan which time-order words to use. Some time-order words are *first, next, then,* and *finally.* You can make your own chart like the one below. Add as many boxes and time-order words as you need.

First,	Next,	Then,	Finally,

 **Tell how to make a telephone call. On another sheet of paper, draw a sequence chart to write the steps in order. Follow the directions below to complete the chart.**

1. Which step do you do first? Write it in the first box.

2. Which step do you do last? Write it in the last box.

3. Which steps do you do in between? Write time-order words in the boxes. Then write the steps. Draw more boxes if necessary.

W R I T E   A W A Y

Use the sequence chart to write a paragraph that tells how to make a telephone call. Use another sheet of paper.

Name _____ Date _____

Writing Pattern: Compare and Contrast

When you **compare** and **contrast,** you tell how two things are alike and different. If you compare an apple to an orange, you could say that both are fruits and both have seeds. To contrast the two fruits, you could say that they taste different and have different kinds of peels. The two fruits are alike and different at the same time.

This writing pattern is useful if you want to inform your readers how two things are similar or different. When you choose this pattern, a Venn diagram can help you plan your work. It helps you think about the similarities and differences.

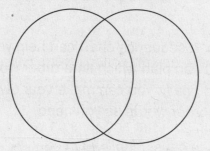

Compare a car and a bicycle. Draw a bigger Venn diagram like the one above on another sheet of paper. Follow the directions below to complete the diagram.

1. Label each circle with the item names. Write *car* above one circle. Write *bicycle* above the other circle. Write *both* above the part where the circles overlap.

2. Look where the circles overlap. Write words that tell how the two items are alike in this space. For example, you might write *used for transportation* or *have wheels.*

3. In the circle under *car,* write words that describe the car. They should tell how it is different from the bicycle. Think about its parts, shape, size, and use.

4. In the circle under *bicycle,* write words that describe the bicycle. They should tell how it is different from the car. Think about its parts, shape, size, and use.

Use the Venn diagram to write a paragraph. Compare and contrast a car and a bicycle. Use another sheet of paper.

Writing Pattern: Cause and Effect

A **cause** is <u>why</u> something happens. An **effect** is <u>what</u> happens. For example, suppose you leave a bag of ice outside on a hot day. The ice melts quickly. In this example, the cause is the heat. The effect is that the ice melts.

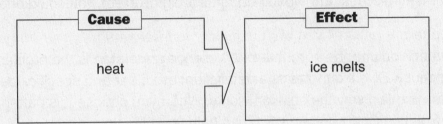

Cause	Effect
heat	ice melts

The example above is a simple cause and effect event. However, one cause and effect pair can lead to a chain of cause and effect pairs. Think about the ice example above. Suppose some cold water from the bag of melting ice splashes on you. You fall back, and your hat falls off. A dog picks up your hat and runs off with it. As you can see, each effect can lead to another cause. Each cause can lead to another effect.

This writing pattern is useful if you are writing about why events happen. You must clearly state the cause and the effect so that a reader can understand the why and what of an event. You can use the Cause and Effect Chart on page 123 to help you plan your work.

Think about a time you had an argument with someone. Use the Cause and Effect Chart on page 123 to explain the details. Follow the directions below to complete the chart.

1. Write the cause. Use exact nouns and verbs to explain the details.

2. Write the effect, or what happened. Use sense words so that the audience can "see" the effect.

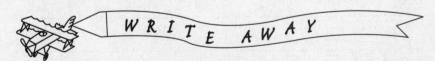

WRITE AWAY

Use the Cause and Effect Chart to write a paragraph. Tell about your argument with someone. Use another sheet of paper.

www.harcourtschoolsupply.com
81
Unit 3: Building Paragraphs
Core Skills Writing 5, SV 9781419034152

Writing Pattern: Problem and Solution

A **problem** is something that is wrong and needs to be fixed. A **solution** is the way to fix the problem. The problem and solution writing pattern is useful to get the audience to agree with your solution. It can also be used to explain something that is a problem. For example, you might discuss how world hunger is a big problem. You could offer a solution to this problem.

When you use this pattern, be sure that the audience understands the problem. Identify the problem directly. Give examples and details that are clear and specific. Identify the solution directly. Explain why the solution works. When you choose this pattern, the Problem and Solution Chart on page 123 can help you plan your work.

Think about something that is a problem in your city today. Use the Problem and Solution Chart on page 123 to list the details. Follow the directions below to complete the chart.

1. Identify the problem directly. Give an example and list two or three details about the problem.

2. Identify the solution directly. Tell why the solution would work.

W R I T E   A W A Y

Use the Problem and Solution Chart to write a paragraph. Identify a problem in your city and give your solution. Use another sheet of paper if necessary.

_____

_____

_____

_____

_____

_____

Keeping to the Topic

A paragraph should have **unity.** That means all the parts work together to tell about one main idea. One way to get unity is to keep to the topic. Be sure your paragraph doesn't have **unnecessary information,** or information that does not belong.

Suppose that you and four friends are playing a board game. You're talking, and everyone is happy to be together. This group is like a good paragraph. You announce the topic of conversation: "Did you hear about the trouble downtown?" (You're the topic sentence.) Three of your friends give details about the trouble. (They're the detail sentences.) The fifth friend just nods and agrees with everyone. (He's the concluding sentence.)

Then your toddler sister comes by. She doesn't know anything about the topic, and she doesn't know how to play the game. The toddler sister is like unnecessary information in a paragraph. It doesn't belong with the other information. When you write a paragraph, always stay on topic and remove details that do not support the main idea.

Read each paragraph carefully. Mark out the unnecessary information in the paragraph. Then write why the information is not needed.

1. The haddock is an ocean fish. Whales, which are not fish, are often seen in the Pacific. The haddock is caught along the New England and Canadian coast. It weighs from three to fifteen pounds. It can be eaten fresh, dried, or smoked. Have some haddock tonight!

_____

_____

_____

2. Cellulose is the woody part of plants that gives them stiffness. Without cellulose, people would not have thousands of items they use every day. Cotton fibers, linen cloth, wood, and paper are all largely cellulose. I'm not sure if cell phones are made from cellulose. I don't think so. Cellulose is an important product.

_____

_____

_____

www.harcourtschoolsupply.com
83
Unit 3: Building Paragraphs
Core Skills Writing 5, SV 9781419034152

Revising

You must write so that other people can understand your meaning. You can probably read what you have written and know what it means, but will your reader be able to? This is when revising comes in. **Revising** means "seeing again."

To revise, read what you have written as though you are reading someone else's writing. Read it aloud. You want the writing to seem new and fresh to you. Ask yourself some questions about what you have read.

- Is the writing clear and direct?
- Are the sentences complete ideas?
- Are the verbs active?
- Are the adjectives and adverbs clear and exact?
- Does the paragraph make sense?

The last question is probably the most important one. If you can't understand what you have written, then your reader won't, either. You have to revise the writing until it makes sense. This means you must rewrite.

Read the following paragraph. It is not written very well and needs to be revised. To revise, you must do more than correct grammar errors. You can add details and change sentences. You must improve the writing and make it clearer for the reader. Use another sheet of paper if necessary.

The best day of my life happened when I did some stuff. That was pretty good. Then I did some more things that were fun. I liked that, too. Almost everything that day was good. I also slept well that night.

_____

_____

_____

_____

_____

_____

_____

_____

Proofreading a Paragraph

Revising deals with improving the content of your paragraph. **Proofreading** deals with correcting your writing. When you proofread, you look for errors you have made. You **edit,** or correct those errors, during this stage. To be a good proofreader, look for one kind of error at a time.

- capitalization
- punctuation
- spelling
- grammar

An error-free paragraph is much easier to read than one with many mistakes. Complete the Proofreading Checklist on page 117. Use the chart of Proofreading Marks on page 118 to help you edit your writing.

Proofread the following paragraph. Pay attention to the kinds of errors listed above. Use the Proofreading Marks on page 118 to mark the errors. You should find at least ten errors. Then write the edited paragraph below. Use another sheet of paper if necessary.

Birds have allways ben part of myths and legunds. In ancient Grease many birds were speshul to the gods the eagle was a symbol of Zeus. The peacock symbolized Hera, and the crow stood four Apollo. Storys tell of birdlike monsters called Harpies and of a huge, terribul bird called a roc.

_____

_____

_____

_____

_____

_____

_____

_____

Name _____ Date _____

Publishing

Once you have revised and edited your writing, you are ready to **publish** it. *Publish* means "to make public." In other words, you share your writing with others.

Write your final draft. Your final draft should be neatly written or typed. It should be free of errors. It should be the best you can write.

- Make a title page for your work.
- Think of a great title. Focus on words that you have used in your writing.
- Add pictures that might help to explain your topic.
- Use charts or bullets if needed to help your reader understand your topic.

If you have done your best, publishing should be the most fun step in writing.

 Pretend that you have just finished a report about birds used as symbols. Make a title page for your report. Include a title and some pictures.

Name _____ Date _____

Self-Evaluation: What's Going On?

In writing, there are two kinds of eyes—the writer's eyes and the reader's eyes. When you write, you see the words you have written through the writer's eyes. When you read someone else's writing, you use the reader's eyes.

A good writer has both kinds of eyes. The writer uses the writer's eyes while writing. Then, to revise, the writer uses the reader's eyes.

A good writer can tell how good his or her writing is. Self-evaluation can help you tell how good a writer you are.

Write a paragraph below. Use another sheet of paper if necessary. You can write about your favorite memory or a topic of your choice. Be sure to include a topic sentence, detail sentences, and a concluding sentence. Do your best writing.

Use the Self-Evaluation Checklist on page 119 to compare your paragraph to the checklist points. Check each point that agrees with your opinion of your writing. How good is your writing? What are the strengths and weaknesses of your writing? Do you have good control of the writing conventions? Do you have good word choice and sentence variety? What can you do to improve your writing? On another sheet of paper, write a paragraph that describes your writing style. Then write a paragraph that tells how you can improve your writing.

_____

_____

_____

_____

_____

_____

_____

Unit 3: Building Paragraphs
Core Skills Writing 5, SV 9781419034152

Name _____ Date _____

Writing a Descriptive Paragraph: Person

When you **describe,** you paint a picture using words. You want the reader to "see" the thing you are describing. In fact, a good description appeals to the reader's senses by letting him or her see, feel, hear, taste, or smell what is being described. The reader should feel as if he or she is with you. Remember to use your writing voice when you describe. You can describe people, places, or things.

- When you describe a person, give unique details about the person.
- Most people have two ears, a nose, two arms, and so on. You don't really have to deal with common details such as these.
- First, give an overall view. Then, give specific details.

    Rudy was known as the strange one in the family. His hair was blue on one side and green on the other side. He had a long handlebar mustache that he constantly twisted. Rudy always wore a black eyepatch. Sometimes he wore it on his left eye. Other times he wore it on his right eye. His eyes were fine, but he said he liked how the eyepatch looked. Sometimes he wore a pirate hat with the eyepatch and made noises like a parrot. As I mentioned, Rudy was the strange one in the family.

First, choose a person to describe. Next, write a list of details you might use to describe that person. Remember to use unique details. Appeal to the reader's senses with your details. Then, on another sheet of paper, write a paragraph describing that person.

Person I will describe: _____

Descriptive details I will use: _____

_____

_____

_____

Unit 4: Writing Forms
Core Skills Writing 5, SV 9781419034152

Writing a Descriptive Paragraph: Place

When you write a descriptive paragraph, write a topic sentence that tells what you are describing. Add detail sentences that give specific information about your topic. Use lively and colorful words to describe the topic. Paint a clear picture for your reader with the words you choose.

When you describe a place, give details that make the readers feel as if they are there.

- Group details in a way that makes sense.
- Lead the reader through the place. Use movements such as front to back, top to bottom, or outside to inside.
- Try to give an emotional sense of the place. Use your writing voice.
- Be sure your topic sentence names the place you are describing.

   Jacy stood silently at the rickety gate of her grandpa's weathered old ranch house. The crooked gate hung on only its top hinge. The house, which had never known a paintbrush, seemed to have turned gray with age. A gentle breeze rippled the tall grass and filled Jacy's nose with the sugary smell of sweet peas. Jacy turned. Yes, there were those lovely white and lavender blooms. But everything else on the place had faded with age.

Think of a place to describe. Then complete the graphic organizer below. Write the place in the circle. Write descriptive details on the lines. Use the graphic organizer to write a descriptive paragraph on another sheet of paper. Try to use movements that lead your reader around.

Name _____ Date _____

Writing a Descriptive Paragraph: Thing

Remember that a description paints a picture with words. You want your reader to see, hear, feel, smell, and taste what you are describing. Use colorful and specific adjectives as you describe. Use lively and active verbs, too.

When you describe a thing, identify it in your topic sentence.

- Use sensory words as you describe.
- Pretend that your reader is looking over your shoulder.
- Will your reader experience the thing as you do?

   Sea horses are S-shaped fish that are about five inches long. Their bodies are covered with bony, bumpy plates. They are called sea horses because their heads are shaped like little horse heads. They can be many colors, but most are brown. Sea horses are an interesting kind of sea life.

Think of a thing to describe. It should be small, such as something you can hold in your hand. Then write a rough draft of your description. Name your thing in the topic sentence. Be sure to include sensory words.

_____

_____

_____

_____

Now revise your description. Have you painted a clear picture with your words? Are your verbs lively and active? After you revise, write your description again. This time, do not use these verbs: _is, are, was, were, am, be, been,_ or _being._ Don't use any contractions containing these words. Write your revision on another sheet of paper.

Writing a Narrative Paragraph

When you **narrate,** you tell about a **sequence** of events. Often the sequence tells what happens in a story. A story is also known as a **narrative.** The narrative can be fact or fiction. A narrative should have a beginning, a middle, and an ending. To write a narrative paragraph, follow these steps.

- Write an interesting beginning. Present your main **character** and the setting. The **setting** is when and where the narrative takes place. (The beginning is like a topic sentence.)
- Tell about a problem the main character has to solve in the middle. Tell what happens in order. (These are the detail sentences.)
- Write an ending. Tell how the main character solves the problem. This is also called the **outcome.** (The ending is like a concluding sentence.)
- Give your narrative a title.

A Scary Place

Tom and Kari slid down the hole and into darkness. The air in the hole was heavy and damp. At the bottom of the hole was a tunnel. Kari shined her flashlight into the tunnel, flicking the light here and there. They couldn't see much. They crawled a little way into the tunnel to explore. A pool of water blocked the path. Their clothes were wet now, and they felt very cold. Tom and Kari turned back. It was not a safe place to be. They decided to tell the police about the tunnel. They would let someone with experience investigate it.

A narrative usually includes characters. Characters are real or made-up people or animals. They act in the events. Before you write, you must decide who your characters will be.

 Write a short narrative like the story of Tom and Kari. Tell about exploring a scary place. First, introduce the narrative with a general statement. Then, give specific details to tell what happens in the narrative. When the events have ended, give a general statement about the outcome. Use another sheet of paper. Draw a picture to illustrate your narrative.

Name _____ Date _____

Personal Narrative

A **personal narrative** is a story about something you have done. Include your feelings and your writing voice in your personal narrative. The purpose of a personal narrative is to tell about you.

- Write from your point of view. Use words such as *I, me,* and *my* to tell your story.
- Organize the events into a beginning, middle, and ending.
- Write an interesting beginning that "grabs" your readers.
- Give details that help the reader understand what is happening.
- Write the ending from your point of view.
- Remember to use your writing voice to tell the story. Include your personal feelings.

A Helping Hand

I had never really met Old Man Weaver. There were lots of stories about him. People said he had been hurt in the war. Some of my friends said he yelled at them when they threw stuff at him. They said he was from another planet. I just knew him as an old man who hobbled around his yard next door to our house. One day, though, I heard a weak cry for help coming from his yard. No one else was at home, so I didn't know what to do. I peeked around a tree and saw Old Man Weaver on the ground, struggling to get up. I immediately hopped over the fence and ran toward him. I didn't even think of what might happen to me. He looked up at me with cloudy eyes and took my hand. I helped him into his house, which was dusty and smelled like old books. He gave me a phone number to call, and soon his son arrived to take care of him. I left Old Man Weaver's house that day with a different idea about him and about me.

Write a personal narrative paragraph about something you felt proud about doing. Be sure to have a beginning, a middle, and an ending in your narrative. Remember to indent the first line of your paragraph. Use another sheet of paper. Draw a picture to illustrate your narrative.

Dialogue

Characters usually speak in narratives. What they say is called **dialogue.** When you write dialogue, you must follow some rules.

- Place **quotation marks (" ")** before and after the speaker's exact words.
- Use a comma to separate dialogue from the rest of the sentence unless a question mark or exclamation mark is needed. Any necessary comma or period goes inside the quotation marks.
- Begin a new paragraph each time the speaker changes.
- Be sure the dialogue sounds like real people talking. Avoid long speeches.
- Use the dialogue to tell what happens.

He Read It in a Book

Grady was a boy in my fifth-grade class. Everyone always thought Grady was kind of strange, but we didn't quite know why. Once, the teacher asked him what the capital of Alaska was, and he said Anchorage.

"No, that's not correct," the teacher said.

"Is so!" Grady shouted. "I read it in a book."

"I don't believe that," the teacher said.

"And dogs fly," Grady said. "I read it in a book."

"Well," the teacher said slowly, "I guess sometimes books are wrong."

A hush fell over the class as though we had all lost our tongues. Grady was sent to the principal's office for his outburst. I don't know what the principal told Grady, but he was a much quieter student for the rest of the year.

 Write a narrative about a person you have known. Include lines of dialogue in your narrative. Remember to put quotation marks before and after the dialogue. Begin a new paragraph each time the speaker changes. Use another sheet of paper to write your narrative. Draw a picture to illustrate your narrative.

www.harcourtschoolsupply.com
93
Unit 4: Writing Forms
Core Skills Writing 5, SV 9781419034152

Writing a Comparison and Contrast Paragraph

In a **comparison and contrast paragraph,** a writer shows how two people, places, things, or ideas are alike or different. You can also write paragraphs that only compare or contrast.

To **compare** means to show how two things are similar.
To **contrast** means to show how two things are different.

The shark and the whale both live in the ocean.   (compare)
Sharks are fish, but whales are mammals.   (contrast)

For a good comparison and contrast, you should have only two items. You should write at least three ways the two items are similar or different.

Read the comparison and contrast paragraph below. Then answer the questions that follow on another sheet of paper. Write complete sentences.

Fish are all similar in several ways, but they are different in many more ways. There are about 20,000 different kinds of fish. All fish are vertebrates that live in fresh water or salt water. Most fish are cold-blooded and breathe with gills. The gills do for fish what lungs do for humans. Most fish have a head, body, and tail. They also have fins that help them swim. Most fish are covered with scales, though some fish have skin. Some fish have skeletons made of hard bone. Others have skeletons made of cartilage. Fish can be almost any shape, size, and color. Some fish, such as eels, look like snakes. Fish are amazingly alike and different.

1. What is the topic sentence of the comparison and contrast paragraph?

2. What are three ways all kinds of fish are similar?

3. What are three ways fish are different?

Planning the Comparison and Contrast Paragraph

Here are some ways to write a good comparison and contrast paragraph.

- Think about your two items. Remember, do your prewriting to make your writing easier.
- Decide how the two items are similar. Decide how they are different. Choose at least three important similarities and differences.
- Write a topic sentence that tells how the two items are similar and different.
- Explain how the two items are alike and how they are different. Give examples.
- Write about the similarities and differences in the same order you named them in the topic sentence.
- Write a concluding sentence that summarizes the similarities and differences.

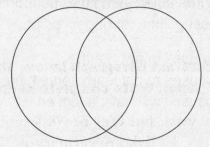

Choose two items you want to compare and contrast. If you can't think of anything, compare and contrast dogs and cats. Draw a large Venn diagram like the one above. Follow the directions to complete the Venn diagram. Then use the Venn diagram to write a comparison and contrast paragraph on another sheet of paper.

1. Label each circle with an item name. Where the circles overlap, write *Both*.

2. In the Both space, write words that tell how the two items are alike.

3. In the first circle, write words that describe the first item. They should tell how it is different from the second item. Think about its shape, size, and use.

4. In the second circle, write words that describe the second item. They should tell how it is different from the first item.

Name _____ Date _____

Writing a Persuasive Paragraph

A **persuasive paragraph** tries to make the reader do something. You may want the reader to buy a certain product. You may want the reader to think or behave a certain way. You may want the reader to accept one side of an issue. An **issue** is an idea that people disagree about. For example, schoolwork can be an issue. Should I read the assigned book?

Each issue has two sides—pro and con. Pro is for, while con is against. State your side of the issue clearly in a **claim.** A claim is a statement telling which side of the issue you support.

Pro: I should read the assigned book.
Con: I should not read the assigned book.

Then you give support. Write three detail sentences supporting your side of the issue. Order your support from weakest point to strongest point.

I should read the book because I might like it.
I should read the book because I might learn something.
I should read the book because I will have a test on it.

Read the issue and the claim for the Pro side. Write three support sentences for the Pro side. Then write a Con claim and three support sentences. Use another sheet of paper if necessary.

Issue: Should people eat chocolate?

Pro claim: People should eat chocolate. _____

Support sentences: _____

_____

_____

Con claim: _____

Support sentences: _____

_____

_____

Unit 4: Writing Forms
Core Skills Writing 5, SV 9781419034152

Writing a Persuasive Paragraph, page 2

When you persuade, you must think about your voice and your audience. You are trying to convince your audience. So you must use the right words. You must know the people you are trying to persuade. Think about the audience you are trying to convince. What does that reader care about? How can you persuade that reader?

You can appeal to your reader in three ways.

Personal appeal: Talk to your reader directly. Use words such as *I*, *me*, and *my* to write your persuasion. Call the reader *you*. Make the reader like and trust you. Use your nicest writer's voice.

I truly believe this is the best way to stop duck parades.

Emotional appeal: Play with your reader's feelings. Appeal to your reader's likes and dislikes.

If you buy this product, you'll never be bored again.

Logical appeal: Use facts and numbers to persuade the reader. When you have real data to support your view, it will have a stronger effect on the reader.

Studies show that 9 out of 10 people don't like math homework.

Use the same issue about eating chocolate. Choose which side of the issue you support. Write a personal appeal to support your claim. Then write an emotional appeal and a logical appeal to support your claim. Use another piece of paper if necessary.

Issue: Should people eat chocolate?

Personal appeal: _____

_____

Emotional appeal: _____

_____

Logical appeal: _____

_____

Writing a Persuasive
Paragraph, page 3

Remember, your purpose in a persuasive paragraph is to make the reader agree with you. To write a good persuasive paragraph:

- Tell your claim clearly.
- Think about which appeals will work with your audience.
- Give your three strongest support points.
- Give your weakest support point first and your strongest point last.
- A good concluding sentence helps a persuasive paragraph. Restate your claim and explain why it is true.

    Water is our most important resource, and we should do all we can to conserve it. We need water to stay alive. We need water to grow food and to drink. But too many people waste water. They use it to wash their cars or water their lawns. They let the water run when they are not using it. They take water for granted. Some places do not have enough water. If we do not conserve water, we will not have enough, either.

Choose one side of the issue about eating chocolate on page 96. Use your claim, your appeals, and your support points to write a persuasive paragraph. Be sure your claim is clear. Order your support points from weakest to strongest. Talk directly to your reader. Use another sheet of paper if necessary.

_____

_____

_____

_____

_____

_____

_____

Name _____ Date _____

Writing a How-to Paragraph

A **how-to paragraph** is a type of narrative. It tells how to do a sequence of events, such as tie a shoe or build a birdhouse. You must plan a how-to paragraph carefully.

- Think of all the materials that will be needed.
- Think of all the steps needed to complete the process.
- Be sure your reader knows exactly what to do and when to do it.
- Use time-order words to make the sequence clear.

It is easy to make a peanut butter and jelly sandwich. You will need two slices of bread, some peanut butter, some jelly, and a knife. First, use the knife to spread peanut butter on one side of both slices of bread. Next, spread jelly all over the peanut butter on one of the slices of bread. Then, place the other slice of bread on the sandwich, with the jelly touching the peanut butter. Finally, take a big bite for a tasty delight.

What do you know how to do? Think of a project you want to tell your reader how to do. Then, think of the materials needed to do the project. Write a list. Finally, write a rough draft of the steps needed to do your project.

Project: _____

Materials needed: _____

_____

Steps to follow:

1. _____

2. _____

3. _____

4. _____

5. _____

Time-order words you can use: _____

Unit 4: Writing Forms
Core Skills Writing 5, SV 9781419034152

Writing a How-to Paragraph, page 2

Writing a how-to paragraph requires careful planning. To write a good how-to paragraph, you should do these things.

- Write a topic sentence that names the project.
- Write a detail sentence that tells what materials are needed.
- Write detail sentences that clearly explain the steps in the process.
- Tell your reader what not to do as well as what to do.
- Use time-order words to show the order of the steps. Use words such as *first, next, then,* and *finally.*

Be sure to tell your reader everything that is needed to complete the project.

Use your ideas from page 99 and the tips above to write a how-to paragraph. Use another sheet of paper if necessary.

_____
_____
_____
_____
_____
_____
_____
_____
_____
_____
_____
_____
_____
_____
_____
_____
_____
_____

Name _____ Date _____

Writing an Information Paragraph

An **information paragraph** tells facts about one topic. You know the difference between facts and opinions. **Facts** can be proved. **Opinions** are just somebody's ideas, and they usually can't be proved.

Fact: The Declaration of Independence was signed in 1776.
Opinion: I think the signers of the Declaration of Independence were brave men.

When you write an information paragraph, include only facts. Do not include opinions.

 Write *fact* or *opinion* to identify each statement. Then tell why you think it is a fact or an opinion. Should it be included in an information paragraph? Write *yes* or *no*.

_____ **1.** John Hancock signed the Declaration of Independence.

_____

_____

Include? _____

_____ **2.** Hancock should have signed his name smaller.

_____

_____

Include? _____

_____ **3.** The Declaration of Independence led to war with England.

_____

_____

Include? _____

_____ **4.** They should have used a computer to write the Declaration
of Independence.

_____

_____

Include? _____

Unit 4: Writing Forms
Core Skills Writing 5, SV 9781419034152

Writing an Information Paragraph, page 2

To write an information paragraph, choose one topic. What will you write about that topic? You need a main idea. Suppose you are going to write about the topic of earthquakes. What will your main idea be? What is your focus? You can write many things about earthquakes. In an information paragraph, you need to develop one main idea about earthquakes. Then you will give details about your main idea.

Topic: earthquakes

Main idea (focus): Most earthquakes are not destructive, but some are.

Details: Many earthquakes occur every year, but most do little damage.

Some earthquakes kill thousands of people and destroy cities.

Earthquakes on the ocean floor can cause huge waves called tsunamis that can flood the coastline.

The worst earthquake in U.S. history was in San Francisco in 1906.

Five hundred people were killed, and most of the city was destroyed.

Choose one of the topics in the box. Then complete the graphic organizer. What can you write about the topic? What will your main idea be? What facts do you know about the topic?

| volcanoes   tsunamis   lightning   hawks |

Topic: _____

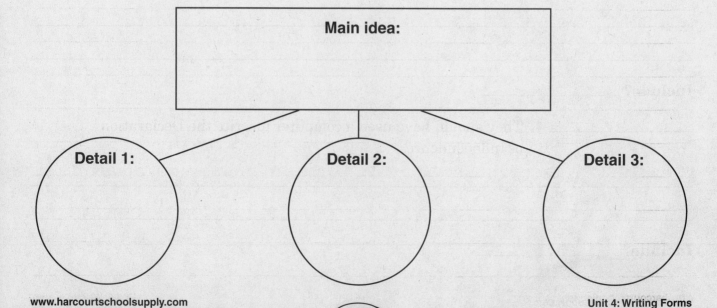

Writing an Information Paragraph, page 3

To write a good information paragraph:

- Choose one topic to write about.
- Write a topic sentence that tells your main idea about the topic.
- Write at least three detail sentences that tell facts about the main idea.
- Your details should tell who, what, when, where, how, or why.
- Be sure your facts are correct. Do not use opinions.
- Think of a title for your information paragraph.

You usually have to read about your topic to gather facts. When you read, think about the facts you are learning. Then write those facts. Be sure not to copy the information exactly as it appears. Rewrite it in your own words. You should also record your **source,** or where you read the facts.

Use your graphic organizer from page 102 to write an information paragraph about your topic. If you read about your topic somewhere, write the name of your source. Use another sheet of paper if necessary.

Title: _____

Source: _____

_____

_____

_____

_____

_____

_____

_____

_____

_____

_____

Name _____ Date _____

Writing a Book Report

A **book report** summarizes the important events in a book without giving the ending. Do tell your opinion of the book. Did you like it? You should also tell if you think other people should read the book.

A Fantastic Adventure   ⌐ title of report

    The Lion, the Witch, and the Wardrobe is a   ⌐ title of book (underlined)
wonderful book by C. S. Lewis. The story is about four   and author of book
children—Peter, Susan, Edmund, and Lucy. They   ⌐ main characters
reach a magical land called Narnia through a magical   ⌐ setting
wardrobe. In Narnia, Edmund becomes the slave of
an evil White Witch. The other children plan to rescue
Edmund with the help of Aslan, a great lion that is   ⌐ main events of book
the true ruler of Narnia. The rest of the story tells of
Edmund's rescue. This is one of the best books I
have ever read. There were times I laughed and times   ⌐ your opinion
I cried. When I finished the book, I wanted to read it
again. I think other readers would feel the same way.   ⌐ whether others should
                                                            read it

> **Think of a book you would like to report on. Then use the writing plan below to organize your report. Use another sheet of paper if necessary.**

Title of book: _____

Author of book: _____

Main character of book: _____

Setting of book: _____

Key events of book: _____

_____

_____

_____

_____

Should others read this book? _____

Unit 4: Writing Forms
Core Skills Writing 5, SV 9781419034152

Name _____ Date _____

Writing a Book Report, page 2

To write a good book report, you should follow these steps.

- Choose one book to write about in your report.
- Write a title for your report. Try to use words from your report in your title.
- Name the book and the author in your report. Underline the book title.
- Name the main character and the setting of the book.
- Summarize the key events of the story, but do not give away the ending.
- Give your opinion of the book. Support your opinions with reasons.
- Tell if you think others would like the book.

Use your writing plan on page 104 to write a book report. Use another sheet of paper if necessary.

_____

_____

_____

_____

_____

_____

_____

_____

_____

_____

_____

_____

_____

_____

Unit 4: Writing Forms
Core Skills Writing 5, SV 9781419034152

Name _____ Date _____

Writing an Informative Report

Are you ready for a challenge? Do you think you can write a report? Keep in mind that your report must be five paragraphs long. You need an introduction paragraph, three body paragraphs that give details, and a conclusion paragraph.

First, you need to choose a topic and a focus. Suppose you are assigned to write a short report on birds. What would you do? You can begin the process by asking yourself some questions. Remember that this is the brainstorming, or prewriting, part.

What am I supposed to write about? _____

Can I write all about birds in 500 words? No, the topic is too broad. I need a focus. I need to narrow my topic.

What do I know about birds?_____

_____

OK, now you have done a little brainstorming. Most work on an informative report is done before the writing begins. There are many things about birds to write about. Let's try narrowing some topics.

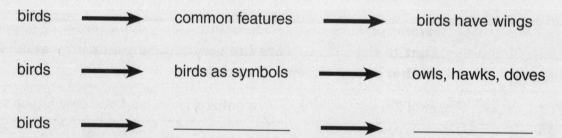

Let's say you are going to write a short report on birds as symbols. The first thing you need is a thesis statement. A thesis statement tells exactly what you will write about in the report. The thesis statement usually goes at the end of the introduction paragraph.

Thesis statement #1: Birds are often used as symbols in today's world.

Another possible thesis statement: _____

_____

Taking Notes

Let's say you are reading a source about your topic. Remember that a source is where you get information. It may be a book, a magazine, a television show, or the Internet. There are many sources to consider for your report.

You find some information you want to use in your report. You decide to take notes. Two ways to take notes are **paraphrases** and **direct quotes**.

- When you paraphrase, you restate someone else's ideas in your own words. You summarize what you read. A good paraphrase shows you are thinking about your topic and are reading carefully.

- To paraphrase, you must first read the source carefully. Then close the source. Think about what you have read. Write the ideas using your own words.

- Copying words directly from a source and only changing a few words is not good paraphrasing. You must write the information in your own words. You must use your own voice and writing—not someone else's.

Carefully read the information in the sentence below. Next, put a sheet of paper over the sentence. Count to fifty. Then, write the sentence in your own words—two different ways! Use another sheet of paper if necessary.

The eagle was a symbol of Zeus, the peacock symbolized Hera, and the crow stood for Apollo.

_____

_____

_____

_____

_____

_____

_____

_____

Direct Quotes

Sometimes the information you find is very important. You can't write the information better in your own words. In this case, you can write a **direct quote.**

- A direct quote shows a group of words as they appear in the source. You copy the words exactly from the source. You put quotation marks at each end of the direct quote.
- If the direct quote includes the end of a sentence, the period goes inside the quotation marks.

  A prehistoric "lake left clay and salt" as the water evaporated.
  Death Valley is among the "hottest and driest places in North America."

Do not use many direct quotes in your report. If you do, then you are not doing much writing, are you? You are just copying what someone else has already written.

Read the paragraph carefully. Answer each question by writing a direct quote from the paragraph. Remember to enclose the direct quote in quotation marks.

One of the hottest and driest places in North America is Death Valley, California. An average of only one and one-half inches of rain falls each year in Death Valley, and in some years it does not rain at all. The valley is the bottom of a lake that dried up in prehistoric times. The drying lake left clay and salt in the center of the valley and sand dunes to the north. Near Badwater is the lowest spot in North America. It is 282 feet below sea level! Death Valley is an interesting place to visit, but you wouldn't want to live there.

1. Where is the lowest spot in North America? _____

_____

2. What is the average rainfall in Death Valley? _____

_____

3. How was Death Valley formed? _____

_____

A Writing Plan: Outlining

You have been using writing plans for your paragraphs. You need a writing plan for your report, too. A longer writing plan is called an **outline.** An outline lists the main ideas of a topic.

- Start your outline with a **thesis statement** that tells the focus of the report.
- Next, write your main headings and subheadings. These parts tell what goes in each body paragraph of your report.
- Main headings start with a Roman numeral. Subheadings start with a capital letter.
- Each Roman numeral should represent a paragraph.

Thesis statement: Birds are often used as symbols in today's world.

I. Birds as symbols of human behavior
   A. Wise as an owl
   B. Proud as a peacock
   C. Dumb as a dodo

II. Birds as symbols of seasons
   A. Robins in spring
   B. Geese in fall

III. Birds as political symbols
   A. Doves
   B. Hawks
   C. Eagles

 Answer the questions.

1. What would be the topics of the three body paragraphs?

_____

_____

2. What would be a detail from the third body paragraph?

_____

A Writing Plan: Outlining, page 2

Read the paragraph below. Then complete the outline using the contents of the paragraph.

The smallest living parts of your body are cells. Although they are the building blocks of your body, you cannot see them without a microscope. There are many different kinds of cells, such as bone cells and skin cells.

Tissues are groups of cells working together. Just as there are different kinds of cells, there are different kinds of tissues. Two kinds are fat tissue and muscle tissue. Each kind has a different function in your body.

When groups of tissues work together, organs are formed. Each organ does a different job. However, all of your organs need to work together for your body to operate successfully.

I. Cells

   A. _____

   B. _____

   C. _____

      1. _____

      2. _____

II. _____

   A. _____

   B. _____

      1. _____

      2. _____

   C. _____

III. _____

   A. _____

   B. _____

   C. _____

Unit 4: Writing Forms
Core Skills Writing 5, SV 9781419034152

Beginning and Ending a Report

An **introduction paragraph** introduces your report. It gives your reader some general information about your topic.

- Write a catchy beginning sentence. Try to grab your reader's interest.
- Name your topic in your introduction.
- Tell some general details about your topic.
- Write a thesis statement for your report, which gives the focus of your report. It tells how you have narrowed your topic.

You probably see birds every day. Did you ever think about what birds might stand for? Many people say pigeons are dumb or crows are clever. Birds are everywhere, and some of them have special meaning. **Birds are often used as symbols in today's world.**

]— catchy beginning

]— general topic details

]— thesis statement

A **conclusion paragraph** ends your report. You don't want to just stop writing after your last body paragraph. You want to let your reader know what he or she has just read in your report.

- Restate your thesis statement in different words.
- Summarize details from your report.
- Tell the reader why the topic is important.

> Read the sample introduction paragraph in the box above. Use the introduction paragraph and the outline on page 109 to write a conclusion paragraph. Remember to restate the thesis statement in your own words. Summarize details about birds used as symbols. Use another sheet of paper if needed.

_____

_____

_____

_____

_____

_____

_____

Unit 4: Writing Forms
Core Skills Writing 5, SV 9781419034152

Name _____   Date _____

Writing Your Report

Writing an informative report takes a lot of time and hard work. You will do better if you have a plan. Follow the steps below to make writing your report easier.

Step 1: Choose a topic. Think about your audience and your purpose.

Step 2: Narrow your topic. Choose writing patterns. Write a thesis statement.

Step 3: Find some sources. Begin by looking up your topic in an encyclopedia. You can also search on the Internet.

Step 4: Take notes. Remember, you can summarize or paraphrase information. You can also write direct quotes.

Step 5: Build a writing plan. An outline is a good writing plan. Each Roman numeral should be a paragraph in your report.

Step 6: Write an introduction paragraph. Your introduction should have a catchy beginning. It should name your topic and include general details. It should also contain your thesis statement.

Step 7: Write a rough draft of your body paragraphs. Remember to use your writing plan.

Step 8: Write a conclusion paragraph. Remember to restate your thesis in different words. You should also summarize details from your report.

Step 9: Put your report aside for a day or two, if you have time. Then read it again. Read it aloud. What kind of revisions can you make? How can your report be improved? Write another draft.

Step 10: Proofread and edit your second draft.

Step 11: Write your final draft. Be sure to proofread your final draft, too.

Step 12: Publish your report. Include a cover sheet with a title and drawings if possible.

Use the 12 steps above to write an informative report. Start below and then continue on another sheet of paper.

My topic: _____

Thesis statement: _____

_____

Unit 4: Writing Forms
Core Skills Writing 5, SV 9781419034152

Name _____   Date _____

Prewriting Survey

My Purpose

1. What am I writing about?

_____

2. What do I want to say?

_____

_____

3. What is my purpose for writing? Explain.

_____

_____

My Audience

4. Who will be reading my writing? What do I know about the people who will read what I write?

_____

_____

5. What does my audience already know about my topic? What new information will I tell my audience?

_____

_____

6. How will I share my writing with my audience?

_____

_____

Blackline Masters
Core Skills Writing 5, SV 9781419034152

Name _____   Date _____

Prewriting Survey, page 2

Writing Purpose and Details

7. Why am I writing? Choose one purpose below and write the details you want to share.

To inform (to give facts about a topic)	Who What Where	When Why How
To express (to share a feeling or idea)	What I see What I hear What I touch What I smell What I taste	
To entertain (to make the reader experience an emotion)	Feelings Strong words Stories Memories	
To persuade (to make the reader think or act a certain way)	My claim 3 facts that support my claim	

Writing Pattern

8. Which writing pattern will I use to achieve my purpose?

Main idea and details   Sequence of events   Compare and contrast

Problem and solution   Cause and effect   Summary

Planning

9. Which graphic organizers can help me plan the details of my writing?

Main idea and details web   Sequence chart   Problem and solution chart

Summary chart   Venn diagram   Cause and effect chart

Blackline Masters
Core Skills Writing 5, SV 9781419034152

Name _____   Date _____

Writing Traits Checklist

Title _____

Trait	Strong	Average	Needs Improvement
Ideas			
The main idea of my writing is interesting.			
The topic is just the right size. I have good focus.			
The main idea is written clearly in one sentence.			
I have strong supporting details about the main idea.			
Organization			
The form of writing makes the information clear.			
My writing has a beginning, a middle, and an end.			
The details are in the right order.			
I use transition words to connect my ideas.			
My first sentence catches the reader's interest.			
My last sentence restates the main idea.			
Voice			
I show what I think or feel about the topic.			
I use the right tone for my writing: funny, serious, sad.			
I use words that my audience will understand.			
Word Choice			
I use the five senses to describe things.			
I use strong action words to tell what is happening.			
I use specific words in my writing.			
I use new words in my writing when needed.			

Blackline Masters
Core Skills Writing 5, SV 9781419034152

Name _____ Date _____

Writing Traits Checklist, page 2

Trait	Strong	Average	Needs Improvement
Sentence Fluency			
I have sentences that are short, medium, and long.			
I avoid repeating the same sentence pattern again and again.			
I use the same verb tense throughout the writing.			
I write sentences that begin with different parts of speech.			
Conventions			
All sentences begin with a capital letter.			
All sentences end with the correct punctuation.			
All subjects and verbs agree with each other.			
All pronouns and nouns agree with each other.			
I use an apostrophe to show possession.			
I use a comma to join two sentences with *and, or,* or *but.*			
I use quotation marks to write dialogue or a quote.			
I indent the first line of each paragraph.			
Presentation			
My writing has a title.			
I use pictures, charts, or diagrams to support the ideas in my writing.			
The final copy is clean and neat.			
My drawing or writing is neat and easy to read.			
I have a cover and title page.			

Blackline Masters
Core Skills Writing 5, SV 9781419034152

Name _____ Date _____

Proofreading Checklist

You should proofread your work before you publish it. When you proofread, you look at your writing for mistakes. Proofread your work several times to search for mistakes. This list will help you proofread.

Capitalization

- ☐ Do all my sentences begin with a capital letter?
- ☐ Are titles and people's names capitalized?
- ☐ Are proper names of places capitalized?
- ☐ Are the months and days of the week capitalized?

Punctuation

- ☐ Does each sentence have the correct end punctuation?
- ☐ Did I use a period at the end of each abbreviation?
- ☐ Did I use a comma to separate items in a series?
- ☐ Did I use a comma correctly to separate a quotation from the rest of the sentence?
- ☐ Did I use quotation marks around dialogue?
- ☐ Did I use quotation marks around a direct quote?
- ☐ Did I use apostrophes to show possession?

Spelling

- ☐ Did I spell all the words correctly?
- ☐ Did I use a dictionary to check words that might be misspelled?
- ☐ Did I use a dictionary to check troublesome words?

Grammar and Usage

- ☐ Do my subjects and verbs agree in number?
- ☐ Do my nouns and pronouns agree in number?
- ☐ Do I have any sentence fragments?
- ☐ Do I have any run-on sentences?
- ☐ Do I have any double negatives?

Blackline Masters
Core Skills Writing 5, SV 9781419034152

Proofreading Marks

Use the marks below to edit your writing.

≡	Use a capital letter.
⊙	Add a period.
∧	Add something.
⋏	Add a comma.
ⱽⱽ	Add quotation marks.
✄	Cut something.
⋀	Replace something.
⟳	Transpose.
◯	Spell correctly.
⫫	Indent paragraph.
/	Make a lowercase letter.

Blackline Masters
Core Skills Writing 5, SV 9781419034152

Name _____ Date _____

Self-Evaluation Checklist

Title _____

1. Did I take time to prewrite and brainstorm about my topic?   ____ ____

2. Did I think about my audience?   ____ ____

3. Did I choose the right purpose and form for my topic?   ____ ____

4. Do I have good focus about my topic?   ____ ____

5. Is my writing clear and easy to understand?   ____ ____

6. Is the main idea of each sentence clear and direct?   ____ ____

7. Did I present information in a logical order?   ____ ____

8. Did I choose interesting and exact words?   ____ ____

9. Are my verbs and adjectives lively and interesting?   ____ ____

10. Did I add details, examples, facts, explanations, or direct quotes to strengthen my writing?   ____ ____

11. Did I remove unnecessary information?   ____ ____

12. Did I follow basic rules for capitalization, punctuation, spelling, grammar, and usage?   ____ ____

13. Did I link events and ideas with transition words?   ____ ____

14. Do my sentences have good rhythm and flow?   ____ ____

15. Did I revise confusing parts to make them clearer?   ____ ____

16. Did I choose a title that grabs my reader's attention?   ____ ____

17. Is my writing neat and easy to read?   ____ ____

18. Have I done my best work on this piece of writing?   ____ ____

Sentence Graphic Organizers

Use these graphic organizers to diagram sentences. You can add lines under the main idea line if needed.

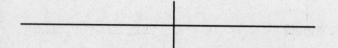

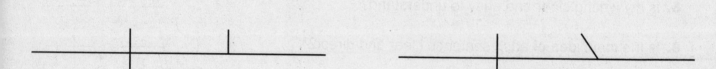

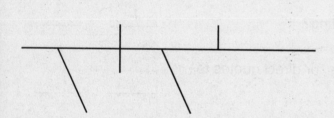

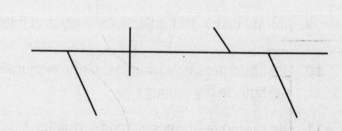

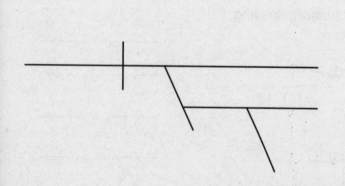

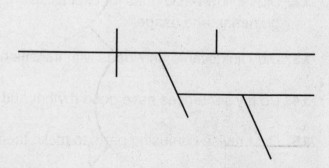

Main Idea and Details Web

Write the main idea in the oval. Write five strong details in the circles. Think about specific and lively words that you could use in your writing to tell about the details. Write these words in the rectangles.

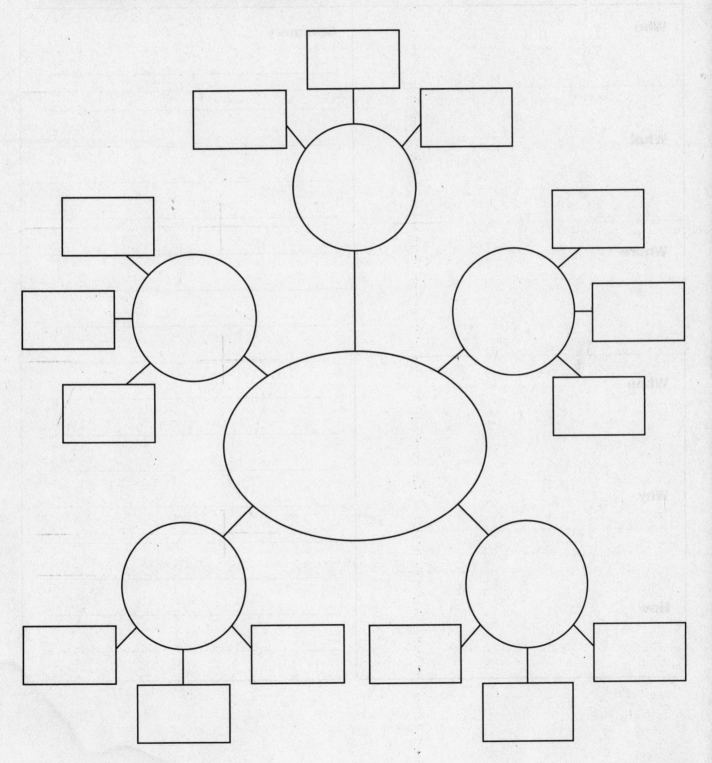

Summary Chart

➤ **Write the details on the left side of the chart. Write a summary on the right side of the chart. Try to include all the information in as few sentences as you can.**

Who	Summary
	_____
	_____
What	_____
	_____
	_____
Where	_____
	_____
	_____
When	_____
	_____
	_____
Why	_____
	_____
	_____
How	_____
	_____

Problem and Solution Chart

➤ **Name the problem in the first box. Then write details about the problem. Name the solution that would fix the problem. Give details to explain why the solution would work.**

Problem	Details about Problem (*Why is it a problem?*)

Solution	Details about Solution (*Why is it a good solution?*)

Cause and Effect Chart

➤ **Write what happened in the Effect box. Write the reason it happened in the Cause box.**

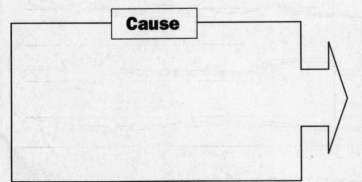

Cause → **Effect**

Name _____ Date _____

Paragraph Structure Chart

⤹ **Use the graphic organizer to plan your paragraph. Write your topic sentence and concluding sentence on the pieces of bread. Write your details between the slices.**

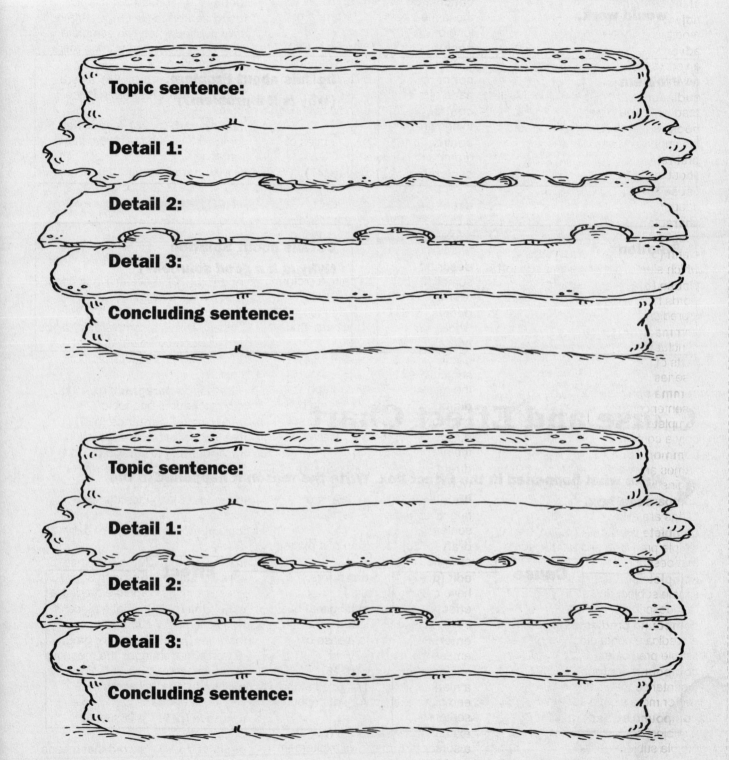

Topic sentence:

Detail 1:

Detail 2:

Detail 3:

Concluding sentence:

Topic sentence:

Detail 1:

Detail 2:

Detail 3:

Concluding sentence:

Blackline Masters
Core Skills Writing 5, SV 9781419034152

Glossary

action verb (p. 14) a verb that shows action

active verb (p. 55) a verb that shows action done by the subject of the sentence

adjective (p. 15) a word that modifies a noun or pronoun

adverb (p. 15) a word that modifies a verb, an adjective, or another adverb

audience (p. 10) the ones who will read what you write

book report (p. 104) tells about the important events in a book

brainstorming (p. 17) to think about ideas for your writing

cause (p. 81) why something has happened

characters (p. 91) real or made-up people or animals in a narrative

claim (p. 96) a statement about which side of the issue you support

clause (p. 37) a group of related words that includes a subject and a predicate

comma (p. 50) a mark of punctuation used to separate the parts of a compound sentence or a series

comma splice (p. 66) a sentence error caused when two complete sentences are joined with only a comma

common noun (p. 13) a word that names any person, place, or thing; begins with a lowercase letter

compare (p. 80) to show how two things are alike

complete predicate (p. 24) the simple predicate and all the words that describe it

complete subject (p. 24) the simple subject and all the words that describe it

compound predicate (p. 43) a predicate containing two or more simple predicates

compound sentence (p. 50) a sentence that is made up of two or more simple sentences

compound subject (p. 42) a subject containing two or more simple subjects

concluding sentence (p. 69) restates the main idea and summarizes the information in the paragraph

conclusion paragraph (p. 111) the last paragraph in a report or long piece of writing

conjunction (p. 16) a word that connects words or groups of words

connective (p. 16) a word that joins parts of a sentence

contrast (p. 80) to show how two things are different

conventions (p. 21) the rules of grammar and writing

declarative sentence (p. 47) a sentence that makes a statement

dependent clause (p. 45) a clause that is not a complete sentence; it must be attached to an independent clause

describe (p. 88) to tell what something is like; to paint a picture with words

details (p. 31) words that tell whose, which, when, where, and how about the main idea

detail sentences (p. 69) body sentences that tell more about the main idea of a paragraph

dialogue (p. 93) words said by characters in a narrative

direct object (p. 27) receiver of the action in a sentence

direct quote (p. 107) copying words exactly from a source

double negative (p. 35) two negatives used incorrectly in a sentence

draft (p. 23) a version of a piece of writing

edit (p. 23) to correct errors you have made in writing

effect (p. 81) something that has been caused to happen

entertain (p. 11) to please or amuse the reader

exclamation mark (p. 48) a mark of punctuation used at the end of an exclamatory or imperative sentence

exclamatory sentence (p. 48) a sentence that shows excitement or strong feeling

express (p. 11) to tell your personal feelings

fact (p. 101) a statement that can be proved

figurative language (p. 60) words used to compare unlike things

focus (p. 71) to narrow a topic

fused sentence (p. 65) a sentence error caused when two complete sentences are joined with no mark of punctuation

future tense verb (p. 56) a verb that tells what will happen in the future

helping verb (p. 28) a verb that comes before the main verb in a sentence

how-to paragraph (p. 99) tells how to do a sequence of events

ideas (p. 19) what you have to say or write about a topic

imperative sentence (p. 48) a sentence that makes a request or gives a command

indent (p. 70) move in five spaces from the left margin

independent clause (p. 37) a clause that is a complete sentence and shows a complete thought

inform (p. 11) to tell facts about a topic

information paragraph (p. 101) tells facts about one topic

interrogative sentence (p. 47) a sentence that asks a question

introduction paragraph (p. 111) the first paragraph in a report or long piece of writing

issue (p. 96) an idea that people disagree about

journal (p. 12) a record of daily events

linking verb (p. 29) a verb that links the subject to a noun or an adjective in the complete predicate

main idea (p. 25) what a piece of writing is mainly about

modifier (p. 15) a word or group of words that changes the meaning of another word

narrate (p. 91) tell about a sequence of events

narrative (p. 91) a factual or fictional story

negative (p. 35) a word that means "no" or "not"

noun (p. 13) a word that names a person, place, or thing

object of the preposition (p. 39) the noun or pronoun that follows a preposition

object pronoun (p. 13) used as the object of a sentence

opinion (p. 101) someone's belief that cannot be proved

organization (p. 19) the way you arrange the ideas you are writing

outcome (p. 91) the ending of a narrative

outline (p. 109) a writing plan for the content of a report

paragraph (p. 69) a group of sentences that tells about one main idea

paraphrase (p. 107) to restate someone else's ideas in your own words

passive verb (p. 55) a verb that shows being and not action

past tense verb (p. 56) a verb that tells what happened in the past

period (p. 47) a mark of punctuation used at the end of a declarative or imperative sentence

personal narrative (p. 92) a story about something you have done

personification (p. 61) giving human qualities to nonhuman things

persuade (p. 11) to try to convince the reader to think or act a certain way

persuasive paragraph (p. 97) tries to make the reader do something

phrase (p. 37) a group of words that does not have a subject or a predicate

plural verb (p. 26) a verb that agrees with a plural subject

predicate (p. 24) the part of a sentence that tells what the subject is or does

predicate adjective (p. 29) an adjective linked to a subject by a linking verb

predicate nominative (p. 29) a noun or pronoun linked to a subject by a linking verb

preposition (p. 16) a word that shows the relation of a noun or pronoun to another word in a sentence

prepositional phrase (p. 39) a phrase made up of a preposition, its object, and any other words

present tense verb (p. 14) a verb that tells what is happening now

presentation (p. 21) the way words and pictures look on the page

prewriting (p. 17) to think about what and why you are writing

problem (p. 82) something that is wrong

pronoun (p. 13) a word that takes the place of a noun

proofread (p. 18) to search for errors you have made in writing

proper noun (p. 13) a word that names a particular person, place, or thing; begins with a capital letter

publish (p. 18) to share your writing with others

purpose (p. 19) your reason for writing

question mark (p. 47) a mark of punctuation used at the end of an interrogative sentence

quotation marks (p. 93) punctuation marks that are placed at each end of dialogue or a direct quote

revising (p. 18) to think more about what you have written to make it better

run-on sentence (p. 65) a sentence error caused by incorrect punctuation

sentence (p. 24) a group of words that tells a complete thought

sentence fluency (p. 21) when your sentences have rhythm and flow

sentence fragment (p. 64) a part of a sentence that does not tell a complete idea

sequence (p. 79) a series of events in order

series (p. 51) a list of three or more words or items

setting (p. 91) where and when the events of a narrative take place

simile (p. 60) compares two things by using *like* or *as*

simple predicate (p. 25) the main verb in the complete predicate

simple sentence (p. 50) a complete sentence that contains only one complete thought

simple subject (p. 25) the main noun or pronoun in the complete subject

singular verb (p. 26) a verb that agrees with a singular subject

solution (p. 82) the way to fix a problem

source (p. 103) where to find information

subject (p. 24) who or what a sentence is about

subject pronoun (p. 13) used as the subject of a sentence

subordinate conjunction (p. 45) a conjunction that joins a dependent clause to an independent clause

summarize (p. 78) to tell the key details of an event or a piece of writing

tense (p. 56) the time a verb tells

thesis statement (p. 109) a sentence that tells the focus of a report or long piece of writing

time-order words (p. 74) transition words that show movement in time

topic (p. 22) what you are writing about

topic sentence (p. 69) tells the main idea of the paragraph

trait (p. 19) a feature or characteristic

transition (p. 74) a word that helps to move an idea from one sentence to the next

understood subject (p. 48) the subject (*you*) of an imperative sentence that does not appear in the sentence; however, the subject is understood to be *you*

unity (p. 83) when all the parts of a paragraph tell about one main idea

unnecessary information (p. 83) information that does not belong in a paragraph

verb (p. 14) a word that shows action or connects the subject to another word in a sentence

verb phrase (p. 28) the main verb and its helpers in a sentence

verb tense (p. 56) the time a verb tells

voice (p. 20) the way a writer "speaks" to the reader through writing

word choice (p. 20) the words you pick to express your ideas

Core Skills Writing
Grade 5, Answer Key

Student answers will vary on the pages not included in this Answer Key. Accept all reasonable answers.

Page 9
1. A
2. C
3. C
4. B

Page 10
Answers will vary. Possible answers include:
1. the writer, close friends
2. adults, citizens, people at a city meeting
3. friends, family members
4. friends, family

Page 11
Answers may vary.
1. A
2. B
3. D
4. C

Page 16
1. a difference between two things
2. addition of two things
3. a choice between two things
4. same as *but*
5.–6. Answers will vary.

Page 18
Correct order: 2, 3, 1, 5, 4

Pages 19–21
1. Ideas
2. traits
3. organization
4. voice
5. words
6. Presentation
7. fluency
8. conventions

Pages 22–23
1. imagination
2. interest
3. topic
4. organize
5. outline
6. draft
7. mistakes
8. aloud

Page 24
1. yes
2. yes
3. no
4. yes
5.–8. Answers will vary.

Page 27
1. flowers
2. hay
3. fish
4. her report
5. me
6. a book

Page 34
Answers will vary. Possible answers include:
1. loudly
2. yesterday
3. away
4. here
5. overhead

Page 35
Answers will vary but may include:
1. Willie didn't want any books. or Willie wanted no books.
2. Willie doesn't want any facts clogging his brain.
3. Willie never keeps newspapers anywhere.
4. Smart people are never welcome at Willie's house.

Page 37
1. Clause: Whales swim; Phrase: in the ocean
2. Clause: Bats fly; Phrase: in the evening
3. Clause: Tessa found the box; Phrase: by the door
4. Clause: The machine came; Phrase: with instructions
5. Clause: the seagulls squawk; Phrase: At the beach
6. Clause: He will fix the toaster; Phrase: for ten dollars

Page 44
1. is
2. are
3. are
4. is
5.–7. Answers will vary.

Page 53
Answers may vary. Possible answer:

Each year, King Minos demanded a human sacrifice from the people of Athens. Seven boys and seven girls would enter the Labyrinth. The Labyrinth was the home of the Minotaur. The Minotaur was half man and half beast. The boys and the girls were devoured by the Minotaur. Finally, Theseus found and killed the Minotaur in the Labyrinth.

Page 56
Answers may vary.
1. acted
2. will act
3. starts
4. will work
5. blows
6. will blow
7. blew
8. will blow

Page 64
Sentence 2 is not a fragment.

Page 65
Answers may vary.
1. I had a turtle once, and its name was Turk E. Turtle.
2. A box turtle is a reptile that lives in fields and forests.
3. Painted turtles eat worms and insects. The musk turtle finds food in ponds and streams.
4. This game is for small groups, and up to four people may play.
5. The player with the most points wins, but the winner receives no prize.

Page 66
Answers may vary.
1. The Grand Canyon is in Arizona. It is about 217 miles long.

Answer Key
Core Skills Writing 5, SV 9781419034152

2. The canyon is about one mile deep, and in some places it is 18 miles wide.
3. The Grand Canyon became a national park in 1919. The park covers over a million acres.
4. You can take a burro ride to the canyon floor, or you can hike along the South Rim.

Page 67
1. B
2. E
3. A
4. D
5. C

Page 68
Answers may vary.
1. Did you see those flying bears?
2. I didn't see any flying bears.
3. In a biplane were two bears.
4. One bear was wearing sunglasses. The other bear had rollers in her hair.

Page 69
Students should suggest that the first paragraph is better. The second paragraph does not stay on topic.

Page 70
1. the nervous system
2. The nervous system is the system that helps your body respond to the environment.
3. Answers will vary but should be the second, third, or fourth sentence in the paragraph.
4. Without a nervous system, you would not be aware of your surroundings.

Page 74
Correct order: 1, 4, 3, 5, 2, 6

Page 76
Answers may vary.
1. sad
2. happy
3. serious
4. funny

Page 83
Reasons will vary but should suggest the unnecessary information is not about the topic.

1. Unnecessary information: Whales, which are not fish, are often seen in the Pacific.
2. Unnecessary information: I'm not sure if cell phones are made from cellulose. I don't think so.

Page 85
Errors include indenting, spelling, capitalization, subject-verb agreement, and punctuation. The correct paragraph follows:

Birds have always been part of myths and legends. In ancient Greece many birds were special to the gods. The eagle was a symbol of Zeus. The peacock symbolized Hera, and the crow stood for Apollo. Stories tell of birdlike monsters called Harpies and of a huge, terrible bird called a roc.

Page 94
Answers may vary.
1. Fish are all similar in several ways, but they are different in many more ways.
2. Three ways fish are similar are that all fish are vertebrates, all fish are cold-blooded, and most fish have a head, body, and tail.
3. Fish are different in several ways. One way is that some fish have skeletons of cartilage instead of hard bone, as most fish have. Another way is that some fish have skin instead of scales. Another way they are different is that they come in many shapes, sizes, and colors.

Page 101
Reasons will vary.
1. fact; include
2. opinion; do not include
3. fact; include
4. opinion; do not include

Page 108
Answers may vary.
1. "Near Badwater is the lowest spot in North America."

2. "An average of only one and one-half inches of rain falls each year in Death Valley, and in some years it does not rain at all."
3. "The valley is the bottom of a lake that dried up in prehistoric times. The drying lake left clay and salt in the center of the valley and sand dunes to the north."

Page 109
Answers may vary.
1. birds as symbols of human behavior, birds as symbols of seasons, and birds as political symbols
2. Answers will vary but should include a detail about doves, hawks, or eagles.

Page 110
Outlines may vary.
I. Cells
   A. Smallest living parts of body
   B. Cannot be seen without a microscope
   C. Many different kinds of cells
      1. Bone cells
      2. Skin cells
II. Tissues
   A. Groups of cells working together
   B. Different kinds of tissues
      1. Fat tissue
      2. Muscle tissue
   C. Tissues have different functions
III. Organs
   A. Groups of tissues working together
   B. Organs have different functions
   C. Organs work together to make body work

Answer Key
Core Skills Writing 5, SV 9781419034152